YOUNG WORDS

Award-winning entries from the
1985 W. H. Smith Young Writers' Competition

D0355834

MACMILLAN CHILDREN'S BOOKS

Front cover illustrations: SARA GRIMES, CLARE DONOHOE,
                            LUCY WILSON
Back cover illustration: KIRSTIN COX

Copyright © text and illustrations W. H. Smith & Son Ltd 1986

All rights reserved. No reproduction, copy or transmission of this
publication may be made without written permission. No paragraph of
this publication may be reproduced, copied or transmitted save with
written permission or in accordance with the provisions of the Copyright
Act 1956 (as amended). Any person who does any unauthorized act in
relation to this publication may be liable to criminal prosecution and civil
claims for damages.

First published 1986 by
MACMILLAN CHILDREN'S BOOKS
A division of Macmillan Publishers Limited
London and Basingstoke
Associated companies throughout the world

British Library Cataloguing in Publication Data
Young words: award-winning entries for the
    W. H. Smith Young Writers' competition 1985.
    1. Children's writings, English 2. English literature—— 20th century
    820.8'09282   PR1110.C5

ISBN 0-333-42124-8
ISBN 0-333-42125-6 Pbk

Phototypeset by Universe Typesetters London
Printed in Great Britain by Anchor Brendon Ltd, Essex.

Contents

Advisory Panel for 1985: Sir Jack Longland (Chairman), Michael Baldwin, Andrew Davies, Ted Hughes, Margaret Marshall and Kaye Webb.

Preliminary Selection Committee: Lynn Barclay, Richard Brookfield, Trevor Hedden, Linda Hoare, Anna Hopewell, Robert Hunter, Timothy Rogers, Betty Rosen, Harold Rosen, Sheila Shannon, Derek Warner and Tony Weeks-Pearson.

Editor's Introduction

About 33,000 entries were received in the 1985 W.H. Smith Young Writers' Competition. The contents of this book (published this year for the first time by Macmillan) are the poems and stories by the sixty-three winners and runners-up. They are broadly presented in themes, and many of the entries have been illustrated by fellow pupils of the winning authors.

There is an aspect of the competition that is not reflected in this collection but is very important to those who enter, and to their teachers. Thirty schools received prizes of £100 for submitting work of consistent merit, and, in addition to all the individual prizes, about 1300 children were sent certificates on the recommendation of the panels of judges.

It is this dedicated and distinguished group of people who provide the heart of the competition. Most of them have been carrying out their laborious task for a good many years. It is sad when, for one reason or another, someone leaves the team after long service. 1985 was the last year for two judges.

Sir Jack Longland, after being Chairman of the Advisory Panel of judges for thirteen years, has decided to retire. He has been a consistent and very good friend to the competition – as has Trevor Hedden, a member of the Preliminary Panel. It is this group that does the initial reading every year. It is sad to report that Trevor died suddenly in the spring of 1985. His colleagues on that panel and the competition organisers, W.H. Smith, will miss his annual contribution.

As this book goes to print, the 1986 Competition is getting under way. The new Chairman of the Advisory Panel of judges will be a long-standing member: the new Poet Laureate, Ted Hughes.

Foreword

by Andrew Davies

> 'Do you feel your throat tightening
> like a drawstring purse?'

> Starlings,
> 'swirling in the currents
> like old sultanas'

> A pig's legs:
> 'four pink crayons worn to stubs'

> A draught
> 'like a ribbon of netted wind'

It's this kind of writing, this freshness of vision, taking you by the scruff of the neck and making you look at the world in a new way, that makes our annual task as judges such an exhilarating one. All the pieces in this book have this quality about them; and the pieces in this book are a tiny selection from a large number of entries – the smoking tip, as it were, of a volcano of furious creative activity bubbling and churning away all over the country.

That clear fresh vision is the first thing that we look for: there are other, rarer qualities. Not many children – not many writers – can sustain that kind of intensity of vision, and control its expression throughout a whole poem or story. But there are some beautifully sustained works of art here, even in the youngest age-group. Look at the steadily attentive simplicity of Ralph Wood's *Tombstones*, for example (I'm unashamedly picking some of my personal favourites here) or Michael Freeman's gleeful grim humour in *My Mum!*:

> My mum knows a ghost that lives in my attic,
> The attic is a cobweb for people my mum does not like.
> She throws them in with the ghosts that live there.
> My mum says don't worry you'll be dead in a second.

Steven McEwan's *A Sad Cat Who Became Happy* is an extraordinary, mysterious poem, blending reality and dream, mother and witch, security and danger, in a complex and haunting way. The author is seven years old, and I wish I could write like that.

In the middle age-group, I particularly admire the exuberant verbal playfulness of Sophie Harris's *Winter:*

Winter is a slipsish season,
When sugarsnow on the ground goes plip . . .

and the sturdy realist fiction of Christopher Turner and Toby Sweet, both of whom exhibit a sense of structure and a command of dialogue that many an adult novelist would envy. In this age-group there are also some subtle meditations on time: Guy Higginson's *The Photo* is the most ingenious, to my mind, and Paul Leipnik's *My Great Grandpa* the most moving.

The oldest age-group offers perhaps the most dazzling variety of styles and subjects. It's harder to pick out individual examples here, but you might look first at the savagely deadpan honesty of Louise Orr's *Flora*, the vividness and sophistication of Bhanu Kapil's *Perspective*, and the accomplished and disrespectful wit of Elizabeth Thompson's *Lucy* poems. And the amazing China Tom Miéville (can it be his real name?) simply boggles the mind. If there were too many like him about, all of us over-fifteens might as well pack it in now.

Where does it all come from? How is it all produced? Well, a few of our entries come from lonely artists slaving away in garret, penthouse, or council flat, but the vast majority wouldn't exist if it weren't for teachers, that much-maligned body of men and (more usually) women, who, in a distinctly unencouraging national climate, stimulate, foster and cherish their pupils' creative writing. They don't get much recognition, or thanks, or money for it. Teachers these days are belaboured with exhortations to get back to the basics (while going forward into the electronic age), with philistine notions of relevance to a largely vanished world of mechanical labour, with reductive programmes featuring 'Objectivity', 'Science and Technology' and 'Standards'. The illusory distinction between subjective and objective thinking was exploded long ago, principally by *real* scientists. The teachers of these fortunate children know that fostering creativity, lateral thinking, imaginative leaps, is not only going to make poems and stories happen. It is keeping alive the kind of innovative thinking that produces breakthroughs in *all* intellectual fields.

'Mrs Hubbard thinks I'm writing,' says seven-year-old Daniel Robinson.

But no!
I'm a policeman chasing a robber.
I'm a monster black and hairy.
People are scared of me.
Oh! Stop shaking me.
Oh! It's you, Mrs Hubbard.

I think Mrs Hubbard knows what's going on, all right.

And if, by the time you've finished this book, your throat isn't tightening like a drawstring purse, all I can say is, it should be.

Andrew Davies, prize-winning author of Conrad's War *and other children's books, is also a stage and TV playwright (he adapted R. F. Delderfield's* To Serve Them All My Days *for TV).*

He has been a member of the Advisory Panel of judges since 1981, before which he was a preliminary judge for many years.

IMAGINING

Miranda Kaye (14)

Arlene McDonagh (5)

I saw a book walking.
The words were crying
I didn't know why they
were crying.
It was because they were all
mixed up and didn't make
any sense.

Tom Hayhurst (12)
Blackboard Scribbles

On the blackboard
There are words, lines and erasures.
Lower down, there is a footprint
A footprint that shouldn't be there.

In the white dusty coating
There are various sub-subjects
A stray 'authoritative'.
Scars of various discussions
Scars that will heal
Heal with the rub of a duster.

Discussions of words
Like 'Index' or 'Literature'
How many times those words
Have been guinea-pigs
Of intense examinations.

How many microns, millimetres or centimetres of chalk
Or perhaps a decimetre or two
Has built up over the years
Years of writing and rubbing
With an occasional wash
Of the mind.

Ralph Wood (8)
The Image Beads

One is a new wind.
One is a fierce fire-throwing dragon.
One is a jealous heart.
One is a sun beyond the sun.
One is a claw of a cruel eagle.
One is a 'hate', the other is 'like'.
One is a fragment of peace.
One is a tree that blooms in winter.
One is a fire that gives heat but does not burn.
One is a clock that chimes every minute.
One is a wheel that turns non stop.
One is a 'like' that protects.
One is a sword that shines in blood.
One is a world of peace.
One is an anger that does not hurt.
One is a pain that kills.
One is a start.
One is a finish.

Jesse Scott (11)
How to Make Nothing

Take away the air that fills an empty box,
Take away the water and the serpents that live there,
Take away fire and the scars it has given,
Take away the land and all that depends on it.
Take away the life that brings death,
Take away night and day and leave us in twilight.
Take away the light that brings work,
Take away the dark that brings rest,
Take away nothing, and everything
And leave an empty space filled with
Nothing.

Jane Thomas (15)

Autumn Gold

'Ages ago, it was – it was!'
Last autumn, when I went to Abbie's for the night.
The last week of our holidays, so Mum could decorate.
So I could get away, to people.
'I haven't seen him since – since we were all laughing.'
And I ran through the deserted and echoing, harbour lamplit
        streets.
Past cold shops and deserted squares to catch
Abbie.
'Yeah. Her dad was mad.'
And over the throbbing engines of bikes, we heard sea-gulls call,
and little kids scream as they flung themselves out over the
        deep, dark dykes on ropes and tree-swings.
'Yep! Jon pushed Smiffy in. I saw.'
Yes, when the trees were softly golden in abundance, the fruit
hanging heavy from its bush; and the sun lowering itself to earth
        in a golden ball of flame.
Reflecting on dykes and golden-rusty leaves, twisted and
        wrinkled by the snow's first icy, groping, long-fingered
        messengers.
'Did I run into his mate? Well, he's okay now!'
When I took the leather-hard, plastic, smooth and exciting
        controls,
And I moved, like flying, with the hard happy shouts ignored by a
        moving, powerful winding-engine.
'No. I did not get the brake and the clutch muddled up. You told
        me wrong.'
And the company. I haven't had company for a long time. I'll
        never forget,
The sun laughing; shouts and moving.
Engines roaring, still winds and intimacy.
'Well, I'm sorry to disappoint you. I ain't seen him since, and
        I'm late for maths. Ta-ra.'
'Say, Abbie, I saw him last night. Up on the docks.'
Saw him just stand, and felt the hurt of a derelict wind, a dead
        expanse.

Great ships unloaded here once.
Is it not funny how little kids find places to make magic?
Places where society is a distant legend.
'You saw him then?' said Abbie, but I just said,
'Don't tell any-one.'

Laura Somerville (7)

I Saw the Wind

I saw the wind,
A graceful unicorn,
A beautiful sight
To see, with her
Horn she pushed
A tree down, an
Amazing thing to
See, she looked at
Me, in a lovely
Way, and then
I rode away
On her back
In a flash
of graceful
White.

Rebecca Hawksley (9)

Jane Thomas (15)

Morning

The sun slants corner-wise,
Light – to light up a thinking time,
Outside, tractors start.
Men in cement-stained trousers,
And boots.
Here, the kettle boils.
The sparrows fight in the gutter.
The radio says
"Corn-on-the Cob is 6p at Covent Garden".
There is delicately singed toast, and strawberry yoghurt.
The shredded wheat packet is pulled to bits for free stickers.
White-dead blossom dances across wet lanes.

Here, it is endless.
The blue walls and ceiling meet – unheard; always somewhere
          different.
The little girl, trapped on a sea of canvas, a curtain,
Smiles at me, an unpaid smile.
Stolen from years of lazy repose.
The alarm clock rings retardedly.
Doors bang.
Hidden in corners are vast pockets of suspense.
Unslept nights before holidays.
Memories of friends.
Pain; and the longest cool morning, yet to break into the longest
          hot day.

Young fears, try to revive themselves.
The Sun.
It folds and tidies them far out of sight and mind.
When the darkness comes, they will grow and multiply.
And swarm out to dance on indigo tiles.

Michael Johnston (13)

Death Recipes

My first recipe is considered quite a delicacy,
in some places I could mention.
All you will need is a kilogram of circular stadium,
two hundred grams of opposing religions,
five kilograms of crowd, one gram of man
and six kilograms of lions.
Then all you do is mix the man and the lions
together in the circular stadium.

My second recipe is rather spectacular,
and though it may take quite a while,
I'm sure that you will find it's worth it.
The ingredients are, a tablespoon of Duke
and the same amount of King, two grams
of claims to a throne and two kilograms of soldiers.
Also a kilogram of ships to take one army to the other,
and a battlefield might be useful.

The third recipe has a wonderful smell,
and I think you will find it very tasty.
It consists of five kilograms of plebeians,
one kilogram of aristocrats and a gram
of masked man, to operate a machine with
a sharp steel blade.

My final recipe is by far the simplest and
is perfect if you're in a rush, although you may
not find it as tasty as the rest.
All you need is a teaspoon full of big red button,
and a man containing no more than
half a gram of brain.

Daniel Barker (11)

The Cat

Her black back shines like washed coal
As she leaps,
Wrestling with a mangled lamb bone.
Madly she girates,
Consuming all the pleasures of a kill.
Playfully it is chewed,
As rubbish in a dustbin lorry,
And the marrow carefully extracted.
So intent is she on her sport
That some unsuspecting birds land,
And pass unnoticed.
Then she stops,
Holding the prey with a tired claw.

Julia Robinson (7)

Animal Magic

Not long ago there came to live in our house a
dark blue Monkey,
light blue Deer,
pink Leopard with blue spots,
pink Elephant with red ears,
dark blue Hippopotamus,
yellow Lion with a purple mane,
light blue Crocodile,
red Rhinoceros,
and a green Tiger with a blue nose!
At night they uncurl to guard our house. The dark blue Monkey
climbs up the drainpipe and sits on the chimney top. The light
blue Crocodile goes out to the garden and lies beside the
goldfish pond. The pink Leopard with blue spots is at the front
door ready to run in any direction. The yellow Lion with a purple
mane stands at the back door. The pink Elephant with red ears
lurks in the garage. The light blue Deer stands and guards the

entrance to my room. The red Rhinoceros goes to the top of the stairs. The green Tiger with the blue nose patrols the downstairs rooms, while the dark blue Hippopotamus stays in the bath. When daylight comes they all roll up and go to sleep, because they are the animals on my blind!

John Plaxton (7)

The Garage

The garage is busy and dirty.
It is noisy and it smells
of exhausts in the dark.
The welder hums.
The spanner bangs.
And the big ramp rattles.

James Pilgrim (10)

Jason Barnett (8)

A Fine Thing to Be

To be a camera
On a leather dangling strap
Focusing tropical sandy beaches.
Sitting on a magnificent lens
Waiting to take a photograph.
A button controlling me
touching me to take a view at a picture
Winking when you press my button
In my mouth is a film of pictures
Like a library of memories
Stored in a giant cyclops brain
People look through me as if I was invisible.

Harry Acton (12)

A Photograph

Surely this is not my mum,
Imprisoned by the sixties' fashion.
Hair too short, shoes too tight,
Like every other aimless teenager.

Little does she know,
That the exciting man she has met
Has come to change her character,
Will make her look at this photo,
Not with pride, but distaste.

For now, she is different.
The responsibilities of family life
Have made her into the mum I know,
The approachable, sensible, maternal person.

Is she really the girl the picture froze?

Guy Higginson (11)

The Photo

The young man stands next to the bomber,
The runway is in the distance
And the trees wave their branches onto the silent planes.
The grey stone walls have the letters HQ on the side
And the watchtower holds the huge spotlight.
The old man hands the medal to the young man
But even now grandfather has not received his medal
And he never will in the land of the photo
As the world of the photo has different rules to ours.

Sarah Blower (8)

Snail

Walking
Slowly along the grass,
The Snail walks on his
Slimy path.
Darkness falls,
Snail looks around,
Nothing can be seen,
Only his slimy path,
Gleaming in the moonlight,
He goes to sleep in his little shell,
Nobody to sleep with,
Nobody to talk to,
All the world to himself.

Sarah Blower (8)

Jesse Scott (11)

A Draught

A draught is a stream, a cool stream,
Like a ribbon of netted wind
That leaves a stirred stillness.

Timothy Saunders (11)

Bike of the Universe

Take metal for the frame and heat it in the depths of hell.
Take lightning for the headlamps and an almighty clash of
    thunder for the bell.
Take the massive buffalo horns for the handle bars.
Take the chain from the gates of the galaxy.
Take the friction pads off Challenger for the brake blocks.
Take two rings from Saturn, use them as tyres.
Use the chest of the hairy Yeti and shape a saddle.
Take the steps into the sea for the pedals and the spokes from
    the huge redwood trees.
Use this bicycle for riding the roads of the universe.

Keith Twine (10)

David Rogers (7)

Fleece

A fleece is sticky and sticks to my hand and when you take it off
your hand has bits of wool on it. The fleece is like a bear skin rug.
It goes rotten after a few years and mouldy. It's greasy too. It
makes me sick. It's just like an onion too. It makes my eyes water.
It makes my heart slow down.

Andrew Farrow (12)
The Starling's Truth

Like clouds of anger
A congregation
of quick to learn fatsnatchers;
But starlings have to eat.

They darken sunny days,
Swirling in the currents
Like old sultanas.

Freckled and ragged,
They are complex and confident,
GESTAPO officers,
the rulers of suburbia.

Trevor Chenery (12)

Terrorising,
Hedge sparrows hastily tiptoeing,
from the silent and white world of
The Bird Table.

There is no sympathy
in the life of
A starling.

David Rogers (7)
Onions

An onion is very strong. It is like a sharp odour coming towards me very fast. We chopped it up and inside were concentric circles and on the outside it was yellow and brown like knight's armour. The taste is like a thorn bush in my mouth and it's nearly transparent too. It is like a smell everywhere in the classroom. It is like an arrow of smell and I am the victim. It's like a mouth full of bees getting ready to sting me. It is a very sharp smell hitting me hard like a pin.

Elizabeth Thompson (16)

Lucy

I

Strange fits of passion have I known
And I will dare to tell
The strangest and most passionate one
That e'er to me befell.

I met her full five years ago,
A gentle girl and sweet;
A dove would settle on her wrist,
A fawn beside her feet.

Round Lucy hung an aura, clear
As churchbells; fresh and pure –
Until, most sorely tempted,
She was caught in Satan's lure.

Her only drink had up to now
Been dew and soft, sweet rain;
But once while at a wedding feast,
She sipped her first champagne.

Her hand moved on: glass after glass
She raised, and never stopped:
Till to the floor, insensate and
All in a heap she dropped.

In one of those sweet dreams she slept,
Kind Nature's gentlest boon!
But since, each night, she's been quite tight
And danced beneath the moon.

II

A slumber did my spirit seal;
I had no human fears:
For Lucy seemed as if she'd sit
And soak in gin for years.

But I was wrong: now in her cups
She neither hears nor sees;
But rolls around and hurls large rocks
And stones, and uproots trees.

III
She is as sportive as the fawn
That wild with glee across the lawn
Or up the mountain springs;
For hers is not the breathing balm
Nor hers the silence and the calm
Of drunk, insensate things.

And when she's ploughed, quite single-hand
And with her fingernails, the land,
And built a mighty dam
Across the rippling springs of Dove;
She slurs some dozen words of love,
Addressing me as Sam.

My name is Will: I do not mind
Her little slip-ups of this kind;
They frequently occur –
A sweet and gentle soul she hath,
Like sunbeams; and besides, her wrath
I wish not to incur.

IV
To please me, for she knows she is
The joy of my desire;
She rubs two trees together, and
Beside an English fire

We sit: she belches daintily
Her virgin bosom swells –
And forests sway a mile away,
While in the happy dells

And in each lush green field, and in
The bowers where Lucy plays,
In every hole a rabbit shakes
And shuts its eyes and prays.

V

She rolls along th'untrodden ways
Into the springs of Dove,
A Maid whom there are few to praise
And fewer still to love:

She drinks her beer by bucketfuls,
And often asks me why
She sees two stars, when only one
Is shining in the sky.

She has a purse well-filled with gold,
A field with several cows,
A little cottage, thirteen hens,
Three pigs and seven sows:

Although on liquor much is lost,
If I should be bereft
Of Lucy as my wife, I'd find
A little money left. . . .

She lives unknown, and few could know
Should Lucy cease to be:
If she were in her grave – oho!
The difference to me!

Elizabeth Thompson (16)
Pythia

I

Sight Insight
 Cold, but not winter.
Men's auras, smoky halos
 Singed, embittered with the firelight
Bloody pink, biting orange,
 Reaching for half-dormant clouds,
Grey, weary, sick,
 Eyes tired and blearily expectant,
Tear-drops like thunder, sad.
 – We have seen it before:
Strange flicker on faces
 Like grisly, wrinkled dolls
Pitted, pockmarked with hatred,
 Lined with ignorance and fire,
Sentiment, huge love of – what?
 We know, we know it.

Man drawn from a desk warm
 With work and thoughts of
Small man's thinking,
 Heavy with Sea's ocean-drop
Of thoughtless, provoking silver death
 Steel-shining, simple, shall I?
Startled! Window, Christ, have mercy
 On a sinner. Me. My silver gone to gold.
Small sound and I feel fear,
 Hatred, hatred, fear, I fear,
Gold eating wall and life of man.
 De profundis, Domine, Domine – O
Failure.
 This weapon worse than theirs
They will learn when night is darker
 And gold and red complete the stitching.

II
Non Compos Mentis

You sat, in the corner of the
                typing-pool
In a growl of voices, laughter,
                mindless sound.
What was it, then, what change
                came in your heart,
Your mind, what took you from the
                daily round,
And drove the stakes between you
                and your kind?

You watched them scutter round
                the candlebase
And you hated them for what they
                were and weren't;
But you envied what they had –
                a common bond,
Humanity's wide wedding-ring
                of lead.
In bitterness, you left your
                words unsaid.

What right have I to force your
                mind to mine?
What right to lift the layers
                of your soul
And brush the dusty scales to
                nothingness
And at Truth's altar pour
                libation blood,
Your heart-bound barrel, tumbling
                rich with red?

O God, what are you, why do
                you infest
With brittle crackle brain
                and inner mind?

What do you say, long fingernailed,
                    soft-breathed,
Why do you flee and leave chill
                    emptiness
And half-grasped phrases
          spiralling behind?

I called you from a time that
                    was not Man's
Some outside lingerer of
          thought and head,
With pulsing temples, thrusting
                    back the life
That, seeking to escape the
                    turmoiled brain
Wails shrill in bursting, twining,
                    fusing veins.

A madness – you or I? Now who
                    can tell?
Which one of us is real, which
                    half-realised?
Who speaks now, who insinuates,
                    who laughs?
Who pulls red shutters over my
                    tired eyes?
I cannot stop you: who am I
                    to try?

III

I watched the casket sinking,
What I felt – it was not grief,
Was not sorrow, was not anguish,
Did not call for flowers and wreaths;
It was simple anti-climax.
I was calm, my mind was cold.
No emotion: empty casket
Death of life foretold.

Some half-caught revelation
Which I was not fit to keep,
Some profundity of insight
That as yet I could not reap.
This long minute was not ready
For the human mind to clutch,
We all try to catch its timelessness
But do not try too much.

Who had died and who lay buried there,
What man of many men?
No one really knows: a name
Carved on a stone, and then
Oblivion. What came before
And what will come in years
When man has found the perfect state
To assuage all his fears?

I watched the casket sinking
And I watch it every day
As the preacher shuts his prayerbook
And the mourners file away.

Patrick Dight (14)

Marie Mower (12)

Lucy Gardner (12)
Pigs

A pig, its body like a lump of dough,
dropped in the mud and squeezed from all its moisture.
Its legs, four pink crayons worn to stubs.
A cork is its nose,
Skewer holes for nostrils,
clogged with mud and sweat.
It moves along through the muck,
its hooves dragging, its stomach wobbling,
like a lazy belly dance.
Its tail a spring, pulled until almost straight.
Dried mud cracks from it as it moves,
uncovering the pink skin,
and small hairs which hold on to muck.
Saliva drips from corners of the mouth,
and trickles down its chin,
leaving a small river of cleanness.

Louise Orr (15)
Flora

Flora died on Wednesday last at the age of fifteen. She was always weird – she could never walk in a straight line. She would stop and start and look around her. She irritated the hell out of me.

Of course, everyone cried their eyes out after it happened. The girls went about with faces like fizz and the boys stood in mournful-looking groups. Even the teachers would sometimes stop lecturing in mid sentence and hastily blow their noses. Hypocrites. She was too good to be true.

'The good die young,' and good riddance. Who wants Miss Prude, Swot, et cetera, around when you're having fun? Looking as if butter wouldn't melt in her oh-so-pretty mouth she'd sidle up to me and ask how I got on with my history 40-Mark Passage.

'I failed,' I'd snap.

'Oh, I thought it was quite easy if you'd studied.'

I'd feel my hand itching to slap her innocent expression but would restrain myself, anticipating the investigation which always follows 'fisticuffs in the yard'. I wish now that I had taken her by both ears and shaken the nonsense out of her.

I have to admit that she was pretty, but in a weak sort of way. Her hair was short, black, and bobbed, and she had good, broad shoulders that were ruined by her little-girl-lost expression and bearing. Teachers liked her because she paid attention and got good marks, and pupils liked her because her dad owned a shoe shop and gave her best mates 10% off. I heard that her dad pulled down rows and rows of shoes and smashed the shop windows when he heard about it.

She fancied me like crazy, that much was obvious. She blushed every time she saw me, but she still irritated the hell out of me. Her stupid pals used to pass messages from her to the morons who were meant to be my pals and a date was fixed up without even telling me until the very day, when she told me herself.

'Hi,' she squeaked. I grunted.

'So are you coming tonight?' she asked.

'What are you talking about?'

Steven McQueen (15)

She looked hurt, but at least had the decency to tell me I was taking her out that night. I had no money and I didn't even like the besom, but we were going Dutch.

We walked along in a dead silence. She circled and stopped and revved up and started again. She was really bugging me, this girl, and I thought about the prelims which were coming up and wondered if it was worth my while to even sit them. I decided it wasn't.

'I bought a Chemistry Revision Guide yesterday,' she said.

This was her idea of an interesting conversation between a girl and a well-and-truly bored boy on a first date.

'Oh aye?' I sounded fed up, and I was. She started telling me in gory detail all about her revision timetable for the exams and how she hoped to get all As. Nothing like a cheery discussion on a topic of mutual interest to get a relationship off to a great start. I felt like running away from her and her mohair jumper and ski-pants. She always looked dazed, as though she normally spent all her time indoors, studying, and was brought out twice a week to take the air. When you touched her head, it felt hot and full, crammed tightly with irrelevant history dates and Latin verb tables.

Suddenly I felt really benevolent and I offered to buy her a slider. God, I hope it won't rot your teeth, hen. We walked down

31

to the river and sat under the bridge. It was very romantic, ahem, until I leaned over and put my arm around her. I don't know what was up with her – she'd been asking for it all night – but she froze, and pulled away. I was really damn angry. I was taking this girl out as a favour – she'd cost me a slider and a bus fare so far, and I didn't even like her.

'Give us a kiss,' I said. She stood up and went to run away, but I grabbed her. I had a desire to see blood and mud mix on her face and to see how she would look with no teeth. She screamed, so I thumped her dead hard on the back of her neck. Serves her bloody right for dressing up like a dog's dinner. What did she expect? She stopped screaming, and she stopped breathing. I wasn't scared. I pushed her into the river and walked slowly home.

Kick

Are you frightened?
Do you feel your throat tightening
like a drawstring purse, with
the air squeezed out?
Does your hair feel as though
it is slipping
Slowly
Off your scalp?
Do you want to run away?
Are your hands wet?
Is your life line distorted by rivulets of sweat?
Do you feel your face burning?
Does it feel as though
tens
of
thousands of sharp pins
are jabbing you?
Do you feel more alive?
Don't say you don't like it.

MAINLY
BIOGRAPHICAL

Sarah Henson (17)

Daniel Robinson (7)
Daydreaming

Mrs Hubbard thinks I'm reading.
But no!
I'm riding a golden horse,
and racing in a racing car.
Hurray I've won.
I'm jumping over a turbo car on my BMX.
Hurray I've won.
The car was going very fast and no
mistake at all.
I'm the champion.

Mrs Hubbard thinks I'm writing.
But no!
I'm a policeman chasing a robber.
I'm a monster black and hairy.
People are scared of me.
Oh! Stop shaking me.
Oh! It's you, Mrs Hubbard.

Damion Rice (7)
Myself

I have got to live with myself at night time.
I want to change my face so I look ordinary.
I feel I look strange like I come from another planet.
People say I'm an extrovert.
Adults don't always like me,
because I'm always telling jokes.
I'm always on the move sometimes I'm lonely
I wish I could be a footballer
because I like getting muddy sometimes
I'm anxious because we are looking after a rabbit but lots of cats
         come in the garden.
Sometimes I'm anxious because I forget to put my recorder in
         my bag but my mummy does it.

Bhanu Kapil (16)

Perspective

In this chapter, we will discuss the self-idealisation of the adolescent self. We will examine the emphasis on social stereotypes and conformity. We will justify the emotional and physical traumas which possess the psychic apparatus of the average teenager. We have a complete understanding of the transitional years. This is not a gimmick.

oh yes, of course i am. of course i have. of course i will in time, i will be me and people will know why i am and things. things are perhaps the most important part of life. they refer to the soft grey insipid dreams that charge malevolently through my mind. forcing me to imagine and speculate. the putty of ambition. once hardened, the dreams will be you. me.
perhaps i am mad.
i would like to think so. it would justify failure and dependence and ignominy and things.
perhaps i'm not really me at all.
please confirm.

Fantasy explores passions which cannot be evolved in reality. For the adolescent, fantasy is a means of expressing the fear and anger he/she may feel towards a possible future. As he/she reviews his/her hopes and aspirations, he/she faces a long, maturing period of emotional re-adjustment.

i want paris in february. a man for the moment. a dream for a thousand rainy sunday mornings.
i want isolation and recklessness.
i want escapade and subtle innuendoes.
i want nonsense and a hero.
a treehouse in new delhi.
discussions on rape, primary schools, and beauty.
i want a purple dress and a harlequin's destiny.
i want bubble gum and summer windows.
i want to build the united nations building in geneva over
   again.

i want to paint it yellow and let peacocks roam its conference rooms.

As adulthood approaches, the religious orientation of the adolescent deepens. He/she becomes prone to professions of a strong faith, feeling guilt at a lesser commitment. He/she feels that religion may in some way aid the maturity of his/her own personal philosophies. His/her feelings are unaffected by socio-economic status.

god is good and kind.
unfortunately, he is not very expressive.
maybe he has no eyebrows.
in all facetiousness, i believe in me.

The adolescent is superficial and facetious. He/she imagines philosophy and depth of psychological outlook. He/she feels inadequate. A compensating factor in this period of emotional instability is the peer-group influence on him/her to take the role of rebel and aggressor. In the conformity of the rebellion, the adolescent is unable to develop feelings of self-motivation.

world, when i grow up i'm going to leave this place and buy a mountain in china. i will marry beowulf and spend my days in his arms. when i am seventeen, i shall divorce him and become president of the southern hemisphere, and then of course my romantic novelette will be published and you will clap. when i'm eighteen years old, i'll build a river and dream of lancelot. i'll dream of you.
i'll be an impoverished piano player.
i'll be a descendant of a mass murderer.
i'll paint pictures.
i'll walk in the woods and jump in all the puddles.
i'll pretend i'm me.

The adolescent has the capacity to research his/her specific animal impulses.

why today?
of all the beautiful, shiny, happy times in my life. . . why did i

fall for yet another older man? his name is johnny and he's a
complete contradiction of yesterday's fetish for young rich
boys. i'm confusing myself – dragging
myself
once more into the quagmire of puppy love. i believe i've
mentioned the futility of it all. please help.

As a by-product of his/her on-going emotional turbulence, the
adolescent finds himself/herself growing in fervour and
commitment towards political and social spheres of life. He/she
grows in self-confidence and becomes clear-thinking and
objective.

> sadly, i am a bungling, indecisive person. i find it hard to
> communicate with the multitudes and, as a result of this,
> retreat further into my shell of insecurity.
> i am naive and arrogant. i am tired, bored and fat. i think my
> legs are blotchy, hairy, and undesirable. i can't sing. i hate
> blue ink. . .
> i am possessed by nightmares, gossip, and jealousy.
> i find the world black, banal, and brazen. fascism abounds.

With the onset of adulthood, it is necessary for the adolescent to
truly cohere his/her identity. He/she must realise and accept
his/her goals and capabilities in life. Ideas and attitudes
pertaining to this realisation have been fermenting since
childhood. This is shown in the adolescent's maturing
emotional outlook on his/her future.

> i am a young girl who has no true philosophy. no viable
> dreams. no practical sensible everyday basic necessary
> logical approach to a long, long future.
> i think i want to write novels about. . .
> i think i want to. . .
> i think i. . .
> i. . . i. . . i. . .

> eventually, the dreamers among you will be washed up
> upon a vast stuttering tide of ineptitude.
> they are, inevitably, losers.

i think i am in an egg. i am the egg. i am thinking: soon, i am either going to burst forth into life or someone is going to crack my head open.
pray for the egg.
the dreams of the millions. . . catch them as they bleed into the night air. i expect they float out of windows and stick to clouds and moonlight and rivers. the seed of poems, debussy waltzes, and adolescents.

Elizabeth Thompson (16)

Manus

Power pulled strength
In this flesh –
Strange control of being.
Can you see, see the
Three-fold pushing force
Relax, float, reach the surface:
Clasp, struggle, submerge in flesh
And nothing left
But a placid, mild sea-surface,
Faint ripples of underpowers
Furrowed, firm, wave-cut
Crashing in crested ridges.
At its ebb
A slow slope, smooth and long.
What shore is this, what sea
That summons me
To shiver and to draw
My gloved soul over yours?

Eleanor Wason (10)

Flora Carnwath (8)

Me

My name is Flora Carnwath, but I am called all sorts of other names like Dora or Sausage and once my cousin said, "Would you like to be called Flossie?" and then I was furious, and I sometimes feel I would like to be called Isobel which reminds me of a bowl of peaches, mangoes and pears and other luscious fruit like that. I really do not know why because Isobel is a common, everyday name. I like spaghetti because it is long and snakelike and twists in different ways. Sometimes when my mother has given me something for my birthday and it is special, then if I see something I really want which somebody wants to swap with me I do not swap it, and often I am so bored that nothing can interest me at all, so I just loll about and draw pictures I do not want to do. Often I feel neglected and I run up to my bedroom and think about the sea with dots of white foam on small, lapping waves and sandy beaches with little flowers of rainbows hues. I love playing hide and seek in the bracken and hearing the crackling sound all around me and jumping on rocks, gleaming among bilberry plants and wet moss, and I love looking out on a summer's day and seeing white, fluffy clouds which I feel I could bounce on. I hate doing my violin practice but I love playing in an orchestra and I hate going for walks on cold, dreary winter days when I am feeling floppy. I like staying up late which I regret in the mornings because I feel stiff and tired and I like cold winter evenings when I feel cosy inside my house, toasting my toes in front of a blazing fire and eating crumpets.

Clare Donohoe (16)

Liberty, Equality, Fraternity – and Justice for All

James Thurber once said that 'a woman's place is in the wrong'. If I could agree with this little gem of wisdom without being assassinated by a demented – sorry, liberated – bra-burner, perhaps I could get a job as Army Relations Officer with the 'A' team. On the other hand, if I say, like Mrs James Thurber, that 'a man's place is behind the kitchen sink tonite, darling', any male chauvinistic porker (pig sounds so tacky) within silk-purse-shot will start digging out his little effigy and pins. The thought of several million deranged trotters beating me severely about the head and body doesn't appeal to my better judgement either. A dilemma indeed – Judas or Jezebel? I really think I'll put a match to my thermal vest. Maybe the grass isn't greener on that side of the fence, but at least it smells a lot sweeter.

Any free-thinking individual with even quarter of a brain cell must realize that macho does not prove mucho. It's high time men were showing a bit of respect for their natural superiors – women.

One of the most popular misconceptions concerning the superiority of men over women is that men are the more intelligent. How quaint! The word 'misconceptions' is very probably the understatement of the century. 'Wild fantasies' is what I really wanted to say, but in the interests of time, space and the guidelines of the Geneva Convention, I resisted this over-whelming temptation. It has been proved medically, physically, psychologically, psychiatrically and even supernaturally, for what it's worth, that men and women are equally intelligent. It's opportunities which aren't. Men have always been preferred to women in intellectual fields such as University courses in Law, Medicine, Philosophy or Astro/Nuclear Physics. This preference is based on the age-old theory of the lesser-spotted educated Porker that a woman will only 'waste' her B.A., B.Sc., B.V.M.S. or Ph.D. by getting M.A.R.R.I.E.D. and having legions of K.I.D.S.

Any lady intellectual who does manage to beat this system is considered about as trustworthy as the Marquis de Sade and is regarded as second best – a poor substitute for the real thing. To your average (and let's face it, he usually is) male chauvinist, hiring the services of a female lawyer is a crime akin to that of selling one's maternal grandmother to the Mafia.

It would be pretty difficult, especially for inexperienced little me, to prove beyond reasonable doubt that all men are stronger than all women. Or vice-versa. Personally, I know some seven-stone weaklings of men who let Cabbage Patch Kids kick sand in their faces and some utter bears of women who're built like Russian weightlifters and could go a good ten rounds with Rocky, the Creature from the Black Lagoon, or God any day of the week. However, having revealed what perverse types I associate with, it must be said that, on the whole, men are stronger than women. You will never comprehend the extent to which it pained me to say that. But wait! We women, by our very structure, live longer than you men and we have one more rib than you. . . each. Of course, if you want my totally unbiased, unswayed-by-personal-beliefs opinion, you can all have your rotten, useless ribs back. . . .

Jobs, like Undertaking, are a dying occupation nowadays. They also make for boring and sensationally short party conversation. This 'boys should be engine-drivers and girls should be nurses' gem of Victoriana isn't exactly aiding and abetting the improvement of the situation. People who take on jobs traditionally reserved for the opposite sex are treated like vampires trying to join the Blood Transfusion Service.

Who needs two heads if you're a female car mechanic? (Of course, you'll be the Angel Gabriel to any handless male chauvinist who happens to be stranded down the M6 with a burst petrol pipe). And as for male hairdressers, they're just a joke, aren't they? Snipping away with gay abandon?

And finally, I'd just like to make a concluding point or so before they put this entirely undeserved straight-jacket on me. Firstly, although I haven't been psycho-analysed recently, I don't think I'm a Women's Libber. If I am, I must be one of the most moderate of the moderately moderate ones. You know – the kind who just toasts her bra lightly on one side instead of laying into it with a blowtorch. As far as I'm concerned, come the next

Towering Inferno, Paul Newman's getting the kiddiewinks out first and then every equal personage can slug it out for passage to safety to grow old and drain the Welfare State. And finally (do I detect relief in your smile?), I would just like to spit in James Thurber's eye, if I may, by quoting a true gem of wisdom from Florynce Kennedy – the woman who is to men what John McEnroe is to Wimbledon Umpires – 'If men could get pregnant, abortion would be a sacrament.'

Please excuse me, my padded cell awaits. . . .

Angela Harvey (15)
'Playtime'

Say grace. Sit down. Take a plate. Wait for the dinner monitor. Say thank you. Eat up. It was always in that order. The dinner hall smelled of mince pie and iced ginger cake, but strangely enough, we rarely had iced ginger cake. Maybe it was just my imagination as my stomach yearned for some real food instead of cold, hard potatoes.

The dinner monitors stood at the head of each table, pouring ladles full of sticky mess onto the plates. I was always hoping that Diarmid would come to my table because he always knew to give me a small helping. Whenever he came, everyone would nudge me and say, 'Is he your big brother?' and I would nod my head proudly.

But there were those awful days when I had to sit at a table full of boys; when we had macaroni cheese for dinner; and when the most generous monitor came to dole out the lumpy, yellow

Marion Beith (14)

liquid which reminded me of sickness. I would sit for longer than anyone else, trying to get it to disappear, until I was the only person left in the hall and the dinner lady would snap 'Come on now!' I happily left my half-full plate and escaped out into the playground, relieved that I'd left the horrible meal behind me.

The playground was big, dull and grey. The building was grey. The shelter was grey. The walls were grey. The railings were greyish-black, dotted with tiny white stones, which we wrote with, like chalk. I cannot ever recall spending a bright, sunny day, or a white, snowy day in that playground – just long, grey days.

Most of my days there were spent battling against the monitors, the Big Girls, and in particular, The Bossy Monitor. I always tried to stay well away from the games which the monitors had organised, but wherever I took refuge, The Bossy Monitor always found me, and rushed over to corner me, saying with a frown, 'Why aren't you joining in?' or, 'Why aren't you smiling?' She insisted on pestering me, making me play her stupid, unimaginative games. All of the girls had to stand in a circle, clutching hands, while two people raced around the circle, then tried to burst through the ring of joined hands. I detested the game and while my hands got all cold, red and sore from being squeezed, I wished I was elsewhere. Whenever it was my turn to run, I hurtled round the circle, never beating the other person, only intent on mastering the art of going round the bends without tripping. And I could never bear the sound which The Bossy Monitor made as she wailed out, 'Cut the cake, cut the cake!' It was a totally stupid rhyme to go with a totally stupid game, which The Bossy Monitor seemed to have invented to prevent me doing what I wanted.

Of course, the Popular Girls seemed to enjoy it. The Popular Girls were usually pretty ones, who liked the monitors and were liked by the monitors. They chanted out 'Cut the Cake!' enthusiastically, and awaited their turn eagerly. In between times, they jumped up and down, cheering, and looking happy and rosy-cheeked. I scorned them almost as much as the monitors.

After a while the monitors surrendered and my best friend, Tracey, and I cherished our freedom. We made up our own games, imagining we were witches and characters in some fantasy story which we had made up. Or else we'd try to walk along the wall as if it were a tightrope. Or else we'd jump on and off the wall.

When we tired of these pastimes, we dared one another to stick our legs inside the small gap between the poles of the shelter, and, even harder, tried to get our legs out again. We always managed to get our legs free, but whenever the boys tried it, Mrs Leahy (the woman with the name that reminded me of leek soup) had to bring out a basin of soap and warm water. She would get really ratty, and tell everyone not to do it again, as we crowded around to watch the operation. Of course, the next week someone would. And the soap and water would come out again.

At times we stood at the line which separated the Big Ones' playground from ours, and looked into that long stretch of forbidden territory, where the older boys played football. Nobody ever dared to step beyond the line. We would stand at the line and yell, first for my brother, then for Tracey's sister, calling alternately, 'Deeeeeeeeermidd!, Liiiiiiiiin!' The familiar faces of older people were much welcomed in this world of bossy monitors. But when they came over, we never really said anything special. The main aim of the exercise was to gain the sense of achievement, of knowing that one had succeeded in shrieking loud enough to cause them to come over. When they were on their way over, we had a great feeling of satisfaction. They only stayed to talk for a few minutes before rushing off to join their pals. When they had gone, we wondered if Tracey's sister liked my brother, and if my brother liked Tracey's sister. Secretly, I never really thought that he did.

But, like any other good thing, our freedom had to come to an end, and so it did when the bell rang. It went with a shrill 'drrrrrrring!', while there was an almighty stampede towards the lines. We joined our particular line and just stood there defencelessly, while the monitors strode up and down the lines, inspecting them like miniature army officers. They stared at everyone, occasionally tweaking someone's hair into place, and always telling Jane Goode to wipe the chocolate biscuit from her face and smile.

Eventually the teacher would come. March in. Hang up coat. Sit down. Begin work. It was always in that order.

Toby Sweet (12)

The Big Race

The day of my swimming race was wet and dreary. I was due to swim two lengths' backstroke at Chester-le-Street that afternoon.

As I walked into the changing rooms, taking a basket for my clothes on the way, I noticed a man and a boy sitting in one corner, talking. I recognised the boy – he was called Gordon Hayes and I had swum against him before. He was fast – his best time for two lengths' backstroke was only one second slower than mine. He was tall with long legs and strong muscles. He had a pleasant face which was topped by a shock of dark brown hair. The man, who I assumed was his father, was the opposite. He was short and stocky with an almost square face and a rapidly receding hairline. I stood still, just out of their line of vision. Something told me I should not disturb them. I heard the end of the conversation, although I had no real desire to spy on them.

Gordon's father said, 'If you divven't win that race I'll really belt yer one!'

'But, Dad. . . '

'No buts. You can beat that lad from Durham.'

'But I can't.'

'You will or else.'

Then his father stomped off, leaving Gordon curled up in the corner, shaking like a leaf. I walked up to him and said innocently, 'What's the matter?'

'It's him. He says he'll hit me if I don't beat you in the backstroke.'

'I'm sure he wouldn't. You are his son.'

'He will.'

'Well, if you just do your best that's all anyone can ask for.'

'My best won't be good enough,' he said hopelessly.

I finished getting changed into my team trunks and, with my bag slung over my shoulder, walked past the cubicles, through the footbath and onto the poolside. The pool was 25 metres long and had six lanes. I walked over to the place where all the other swimmers from Durham had gathered and let my bag fall heavily onto a bench. Then I strolled over to Lane One and dived in. The water felt freezing – so cold I could hardly breathe. I swam up and down vacantly for a few lengths, my mind always thinking about one thing – Gordon Hayes and his father's threats if he did not win the race. I came out of my reverie to hear a voice shouting my name. I looked up to see the club coach standing on the poolside calling to me to come and do a timed one length sprint to see if I was fully loosened out. I swam to the end and crouched in the backstroke start position.

The coach barked, 'Take your marks.'

I tensed.

'Go!'

I pushed off from the side with a flurry of water kicked by my feet. My back dive had left me about one foot under the water so I kicked to the surface and started using my arms as well as my legs. I swam as fast as I could for the other end and when my hand hit the end, the coach's finger hit the 'stop' button on the stopwatch. He looked at my time.

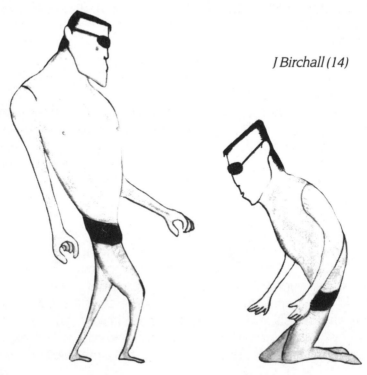

J Birchall (14)

'Hmmmm. 15.74 seconds. That's good. Go and put your tracksuit on and keep warm. You don't swim till the fifth event.'

I walked over to my bag and took out my towel and tracksuit. I dried myself off, put on my tracksuit and sat down. I made myself as comfortable as I could – I sat on my towel to ease the hardness of the bench and leant against my near empty bag to relax until my race. All the heats preceding mine passed one after the other as if only one race was being swum again and again. The coach approached me and said, 'It's nearly time for your race so you had better do some loosening exercises.'

I got up slowly and began to swing my arms to loosen them out. Then I bent over and touched my toes ten times to loosen my stomach muscles and the backs of my legs. I sat down again and went over the coming race in my mind, to plan my strategy. Then I remembered Gordon Hayes. I saw a picture in my mind of his father raising his fist. I tried to concentrate on the race but I found that I could not.

At last it was time for the race. I stood behind the starting block of Lane Three as a woman came to each swimmer in turn and took their entry cards so that their times could be recorded. As she came up to me I held out my card ready. I looked along the line of swimmers but I did not know any of them except Gordon Hayes who was in Lane 4, next to me.

The starter blew his whistle for silence and told us to jump into the water. I jumped in last and went down to the bottom, gave a big kick and was up to the surface again. I caught hold of the side just as the starter said, 'Take your marks.'

Again I tensed waiting for the gun. When it came the line of swimmers all did a back dive away from the wall. I did not go as deep as I had in the warm-up so I did not have to kick as hard to reach the surface. It was only two lengths so I started swimming flat out straight from the start. I looked up and saw the flags which meant that I was near to the end of the first length. My left hand found the wall. I spun my body round on my back, flicked my legs over and pushed off from the side. As I surfaced I quickly glanced at the spectators' gallery. There I saw Mr Hayes shouting at Gordon to go faster. I looked to my left and saw Gordon only a half of a body behind. No one else was anywhere near us. Again I saw the flags and behind them Mr Hayes's shouting mouth and threatening fist. I slowed down and saw Gordon catch up and swim past me to finish a split second ahead. I climbed out of the water, panting heavily, and shook Gordon's hand.

The officials lost no time in presenting us with our medals. As I stood on the second place block and looked up to see Gordon on the winner's block I felt a sharp pang of regret that I had let him win. However, when I looked up to the spectators' gallery and saw Mr Hayes smiling for once in his life I thought it was worth it.

I was wrong. As we were walking away from the podium Gordon turned to me with an unpleasant sneer on his face and said, 'You're pathetic, I beat you by miles. I don't know how you ever beat me before. Well, you're never going to again. So there!'

Christopher Turner (13)
The First and Last Round of a Fight

'You go in goal for a change,' I said to Edward, my best friend. 'It's boring.'

'It's my garden, and it is my football, so there,' said Edward as he stuck a huge tongue out at me from a chocolate-covered mouth.

This started one chilly winter's morning; Edward and I had decided to have a game of football in his garden. I soon became very angry, because of what he had done to me. I stuck my tongue out, thinking to myself that I was exceptionally brave. Sticking your tongue out was the worst thing you could do when I was four. You would never do it to a grown-up, it was such a terrible thing.

'You are a flid!' he shouted. 'You can't even kick the ball, let alone save a very simple shot from me.' He shot at the goal made from jackets placed on the ground. He had made it very large, and he knew he had. He just wanted to make me look bad at football. The shot went wide. 'What a goal!' he shouted. 'I am tons better than you!'

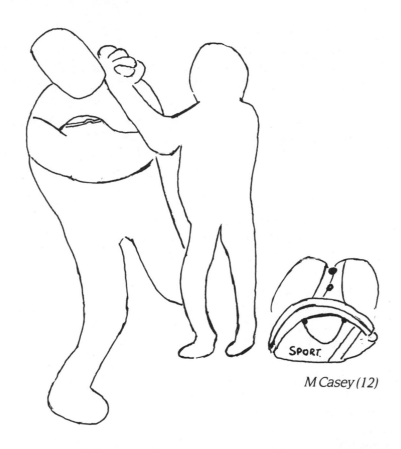

M Casey (12)

I had just remembered what he had said about me before.
'What is a flid?' I thought to myself. I did not want to ask him, or I
would get embarrassed. 'That went a mile wide,' I said, 'and you
are no good at football either. You are terrible.'

'Don't say things like that about me, son!' he shouted, trying
to look tough by putting on a Geordie accent, 'or I'll kick your
head in, son.' I thought he sounded pathetic. He came towards
me, and pushed his fist against my face, not hitting me.

'Don't!' I replied, shouting at the top of my voice.

'Are yu gunno make us, son?' he said, pushing his fist
against my head once more. I became angry. 'Yes, I am!' I
shouted. He kicked me on the knee. I didn't reply to his kick,
because, as I was staying at his house for the night, I had to keep
on goodish terms with him.

'Yu frightened, aren't ya!' he shouted. 'What a baby!'

'No I'm not!' I shouted back. I really was frightened of him because I thought he was much stronger than I was, but I did not want to show it. 'I am older than you anyway, so I can boss you around.' I could see that he could not answer this. He suddenly lashed out at my face with his dirty fist. I dodged his blow smartly; I laughed with joy. I tried to show him I was stronger than him by standing there with my arms folded. I stuck my tongue out at him again. He went bright red, and he once more lashed out at my face. I was too busy sneering at him to notice this. His blow hit me. 'Sod!' I shouted. I, for the first time in my life, hit Edward on the face. I was shocked to see Edward fall to the ground. He started to cry. Edward quickly stood up and shouted, 'Get out of *my* house!' He stopped talking in a Geordie accent.

'I won't, so there.' I once again stuck my tongue out. Punches flew, legs were kicked and hair was pulled. Edward ended up on the ground. I felt victorious, but somehow frightened; it was my best friend on the ground. Even so, I sat on his chest and pinned his weary arms down. My face was stinging, my legs were sore, and my nose was bloody. Having a bleeding nose for the first time made me feel more confident. I also started crying. For the first time in my life I had fought somebody. Before this, I had always been afraid; but this time my anger blew up, like a volcano that desperately wanted to get its lava out. I felt sorry for Edward, for he was crying. I stood up, and tried to show that I was unhurt by running with the football. Underneath I was not unhurt. Edward got up and said, 'Get out, flid; get out of *my* garden. You are just a poor tramp. You can't afford a good car, *tramp.*' I ignored him, and walked towards my jacket that was on the ground. He kept shouting at me, but I still ignored him. He became very irritated, and he walked towards his house; he went in. I stayed outside for five mintues; I felt guilty. I once again started to cry; I walked towards Edward's house, and I told his mum what had happened; she understood.

A few minutes later Edward and I made up; he said he was sorry; I also apologised.

Since that day we have hardly ever fought or argued. We are still best of friends after eleven years.

Kevin Wright (14)

Piano, No Piano

A long while ago,
Before the arthritis,
There was a sound,
The sound of a piano,
A nice sound.

Then came another sound,
The sound of a lorry,
The voices.
"Allo Bill.'
"Allo Alf.'
'Got this piano inside.'
'Can you take it away?'
'Yeah but not like that. Smash it up.'

Then more sound,
The sound of splintering wood,
The sound of a piano,
But not a nice sound,
The last sound it would make as a piano.

Then again the sound of the lorry,
"Allo Alf.'
'Load it in.'
Then the sound of junk,
Not a piano
Junk

In my mind,
I thought it was such a shame,
A beautiful piano
Even though I had not set eyes on it,
Why?
Why smash it up?
Why not sell it?
Then you would profit,
So would whoever's bought it,
Anyway too late now.

Guy Burt (12)

Unsuspected Hero

I really can't think of anyone whom I would like to be less than Jossy Pherit. To begin with, what about the name? And his dad – oh yes, his dad! Apart from providing employment for the constabulary he was of no use to the community.

Even so, I like Jossy. He is one of nature's bad examples; a warning to humankind. He was quite illiterate. He went to school once – not that that proves anything, though. Anyway, it all happened when we were fishing.

I'd got hold of the boat; the one Andy used to moor up by the Old Huts. We often went up by the Old Huts – there were good fish in the river there. The boat was just watertight, and it was this relic we made use of on our fishing excursions.

Joss turned up late, with such a set of tackle you wouldn't see on a trout stream in the highlands. Green, it was; dark green, with little black rings and gauges and handles sprouting from it.

'Where in heaven did you get that?' asked the third member of our group, enviously. He was a young and inexperienced boy, who had been lumbered on us by his mother. 'Do take little Theodore with you, boys'; you know.

Jossy looked proud, and said nothing. And so we set out.

The boat took in some water, but it held together. Fishing was bad; even Jossy's real triple-hook-spinner didn't catch anything. Looking at him he was a strange sight; long, grainy black hair, and a wild light in his eyes. Subdued, though: that came from having a father like a sledgehammer.

He never did a thing right in his life. You name it, Jossy Pherit couldn't do it. Oh, except swim.

He could swim. Well, it came naturally – he learned at an early age that the only way to escape when thrown into the river is to swim across to the other side and go home.

'Hey look, blackb'ries!' yelled Joss. When I looked, sure enough there was a bush – no, two bushes – both laden.

'Stop the boat!' I cried, poling us frantically towards the bank.

'I want to fish,' said Ted, sullenly.

'I want blackb'ries,' said Jossy. I agreed.

'You stay here and fish,' we said. He did.

Those blackberries were good, no denying it. Time flew, and we were soon walking back to the boat, pockets dripping with succulent fruits.

The boat had gone.

That is a phrase that gives no idea of the sheer terror that seized us – only four miles down was Millerson's Weir, and the current was fast.

'God!' I was rooted. By the time my stomach had stopped trying to crawl up my throat, Jossy was gone too. I could see him, maybe two hundred yards down the bank, running.

It was the first time I had ever dialled the famous '999' call. 'Police, please', I said. No one the other end seemed disturbed. They asked where I was, what had happened – it took a long time.

Not knowing what was going to happen, I went back to the river. There was a huge crowd on the bank; word had spread.

In the turbulent, knotty waters was the boat, being thrown to and fro, in it Ted. And clutching it, pulling it to land: JOSSY! I couldn't believe my eyes. This son of a drunkard, wimp of Warlshaw – saving a lad's life less than five hundred yards from the weir.

For the second time in an hour, my stomach did acrobatics. No one had ever survived once they were in that stretch of water. It was said that the mud harboured the bones of no less than seven men.

And here was Joss, swimming against the current with a boat behind him.

His reception was immense. Mrs Ted had hysterics, there were at least four policemen and even Joss's father turned up – in a foul temper.

Joss was on the telly, too. He was there with his father, who kept saying 'Oh yesh, he'sh a fine boy,' and ruffling Joss's hair. Joss looked very uncomfortable.

And the papers. *Amazing Child Hero Saves Boy From Certain Death*, read the headlines. New-found friends flocked to the Pherit household.

But soon everything was back to normal. The short-term associates retreated into the background, and I had a chance to ask Joss what had happened. 'Why on earth did you do it, Jossy?' I asked. 'I wouldn't 'a' dared.' He looked guilty, and finally leant forward, and said, confidingly: 'Well, I'd borrowed my dad's fishing tackle, hadn't I? Couldn't let that go over the weir. . . .'

UNSUSPECTED HERO.

Sarah Watkins (12)

Trouble at Home!

As my father said, money was our only problem and it was a big problem. Money could lead to our success or our failure. At the moment it was leading to our failure. Ever since Dad had lost his job at Midland Bank we had been having problems. For instance, the mortgage on our large house in a very well-to-do area was far too large for the amount of dole money he was given. So in the end it was inevitable. We had to move. We moved into a council house on a London housing estate. I was perfectly happy living there. True, I didn't have as many clothes as I would have liked, but then no one does, do they?

This style of living was fine, until the day Mum became a spendthrift! Sounds funny doesn't it? Well, we didn't think it was very funny when we received letters threatening to cut off our electricity, our telephone, our water, etc. And *then* Dad found out that Mum was using the money set aside for bills to buy a new pair of shoes every week! He nearly hit the roof. So did Mum.

He said that she ought to be adult enough to realise the situation they were in. She said that if it hadn't been for him and his lousy bank they wouldn't have been in this 'situation' at all!

They continued like this until I went to bed. Then they paused for a while and started again. This time it was worse. Later there was a long silence. Then from downstairs I heard my father yell, 'Here you are. . . yes, money, money! . . . You know, it comes in notes and coins! . . . Yes, it's for you. Now get out of my house and spend it on your beloved clothes and shoes!'

A few minutes later I heard the door slam and footsteps crunching across the gravel. The stairs creaked as my dad made his way laboriously up the stairs. I turned my face into the pillow and cried myself to sleep.

When I woke up my father was still asleep, lying fully clothed on top of the bed. It was Monday, and, as usual, a school day. I then walked into my younger brothers' bedroom. They were twins and I stood gazing down sadly at the two blond heads, with their bedclothes tangled up and in a mess at the far end of the bed. I felt so sorry for them. I mean at one and a half years old they wouldn't have understood the shouting downstairs last night. They wouldn't understand anything, except that their mother had suddenly disappeared. They wouldn't even know if she was going to come home again. Come to think of it, neither did I.

After deciding not to wake them I went downstairs, had breakfast, and went to school leaving a note for my father on the coffee table to tell him where I had gone. I didn't want to leave the twins and Dad alone, but I thought, as I trudged off to school, that if we were going to live without Mum *someone* had to go on as usual.

School was as usual except I could not concentrate. All the time the same four things kept popping in and out of my mind. Mum, Dad, Tom and Tim (the twins), Mum, Dad, Tom and Tim. Mum, Dad, Tom and Tim. Over and over those four names raced through my head.

Later that day I arrived home to find an empty house. I made myself a cup of tea, sat down in an armchair and sobbed quietly to myself until I fell asleep.

I woke up and found it was 1.00 a.m. Still nobody was home. What was I going to do? We had only recently moved into the area, so there was no one I knew well enough to call on at this time in the morning! Well. . . I could call the police, I mused. Yes! The police! They were bound to help me. I rang the police and told them what had happened. I also told them that I wouldn't have been so worried if Dad had left the twins at home. Then they asked me if there had been any emotional upsets in the family lately. I told him about my mother leaving. He sounded slightly sympathetic but still continued questioning me. Lastly he asked me how old I was. I told him I was eleven years old. He then told me that someone would come round to take me to the station.

I sat in the armchair and waited. After about fifteen minutes a woman police constable arrived to take me to the police station. Before we departed she left a note to tell my father where I had gone and asking him to call at the police station and collect me on his return.

She was extremely kind and reassuring and when we arrived I was sat on a chair in a kind of waiting room with a policeman behind the desk. A few minutes later the same policewoman

Lucy Williams (11)

the other lived in East Germany! She wouldn't go to nan and grandad either as she didn't get on with them at all. Who would emerged from a room that looked like a kitchen with a steaming hot cup of soup. She gave it to me saying, 'You must be starving. Here, drink this!'

I obediently sat, thankfully sipping the soup and answering her questions between sips.

The only question I really had to think about was the last one she asked, 'Where do you think your mother will have gone?' I sat and pondered for a while on this question. Well! She wouldn't have gone to her mother and father. After all, one was dead and she go to? Maybe a friend. Denise or Rosemary or. . . *Rosemary!* That was it. She would have gone to Rosemary's.

When I told the policewoman that Mum would have gone to Rosemary's the policewoman smiled and asked me,'Rosemary who?' and did I know where she lived? Did I know her telephone number? I told her 'Yes,' I knew where she lived. No, I didn't know her telephone number and her surname was Stanbridge.

After finding Rosemary's 'phone number the policeman behind the desk rang her up to ask if my mother was there. When he came off the 'phone he came across to me and explained that although my mother was at Rosemary's she was not going to come and collect me. Then he made more enquiries, not about my mother this time, but about my father. While the policewoman chatted to me about this and that, I found that I could no longer really take in what she was saying. I had finished my soup now and was content to let the cup fall to the floor and lie back in the chair - asleep.

When I awoke I found I was still in the chair but there was a lovely, warm blanket draped over me. I felt a bit stiff, but refreshed. A policeman appeared smiling from the kitchen with a cup of tea and asked me if I wanted any breakfast. I declined the kind offer of breakfast, but gratefully drank the tea he brought me. Then he left the room.

A minute or two later a different policewoman from the first entered the room. She didn't look very happy and what she said wasn't exactly exhilarating either. She said, quite bluntly, 'I am sorry, but there is some bad news to tell you. We think it would be better for someone whom you know to break this news to you, so your mother has consented to come over.'

I supposed she thought I would cry or be happy or something, but, I thought to myself, too many bad things had happened lately for me to be particulary worried about this 'bad news'!

Approximately a quarter of an hour later my mother appeared and I only had to look at the pain in her red, swollen eyes to realise what had happened, and, as I ran into my mother's outstretched arms, I knew, somehow, that she would never leave me again.

Steven McEwan (7)

A Sad Cat Who Became Happy

Black cats, white cats
Ginger cats all in a box.
The witch is head of us all.

My name is Batermener
I come from Germany
I live in this OLD OLD box.

His name is Georgie
He comes from England
He lives in that NEW NEW box

I am very lonely.

My box is made of cardboard
Theirs is made of wood

I am very lonely
because he lives with the others for company.

THERE ARE RAGS IN MINE
AND THERE IS HAY IN THEIRS.

I am a kitchen cat in my dream.
I sit by the fire
all contented and fat.

The witch came in last night.
She gnashed her teeth.
We tried to sleep.

When the children go to bed
I sit on the mother's lap
Feeding from her hand.

She poked our bones
She pulled our fur
We pretended to sleep.

I am their pet
I am their favourite
I watch the baby
lest it wakes.

She lifted her stick

I ran away.

Come here little cat
Come and get a saucer of milk.
I've got a happy home.

My name is Batermener.
I come from Germany
I have a very happy home.

Emily-Kate Johns (12)

I Am What I Am

I haven't any friends. I'm sly and disliked. My cruelty ranges from slight to magnificent. I like to crouch low, so I'm barely recognisable. Everyone will let me go my own way, for if they don't. . . if there's no one to tease, I sometimes pretend and play my own games, responding to the movements of my body, as if it were a puppet moved by invisible strings. The slightest possibility of being able to torture gives me the patience to sit still for hour upon hour. I like to fight flesh and blood, though trees provide fascinating practice. The tall grasses hide my silhouette as I stealthily creep towards my prey. If a mouse dares to rush across my path it will be dead with blood running from its neck, within seconds. I may appear lazy at times, when I stretch and bask in the sun, but the slightest whisper, and I will be alert, ready to pronounce death. My sense of direction is the finest ever known. After wandering for miles I shall be back in time to frighten one last victim, before daybreak.

I insist on entering my home at eight o'clock a.m. precisely, and if my family do not open the door to let me in at once, I will protest loudly until they obey me. I always walk nonchalantly and demand my food (which must be nothing but the best). I make it perfectly clear that I require my meal on a spotless plate. It must be beautifully designed, with delicate engravings. I must have the honour of eating first, while others look at me affectionately. I can eat what I like, but sometimes I let them decide on what calories I have in my food. A contemptible mouse may show off to its friends, and run under my nose, but I, knowing better, shall just wave it away with a disdainful sneer. I demand my priority to sit in the most comfortable chair, and finest goosedown cushions provide the only acceptable seat. If I don't get my way, I will sit in the middle of the carpeted floor with my back turned on everyone, making it obvious that I won't stop sulking until they give up my seat. Then I relax and my eyes gradually close. . . . But do not make the mistake of thinking that I'm asleep.

Strolling along the outskirts of literature and bio-chemistry, I feel deep satisfaction well up inside me. Although I have no need of them now (for I am too clever), books still hold a great deal of curiosity beneath their mysterious covers. I find the small but convenient library in our household well supplied with education, although, I am sorry to say, some people take it too much for granted. I do not like to be disturbed while I am studying the shades of the binding on the books, or when I am just pawing over the shelves, though a friend to confide in is a pleasurable occasion. Mice often poke their little brown, twitching heads through a gap in the never-ending rows of books, just to see what I am doing. I sneak a look at them (without being seen) and then I shall cleverly smile, and walk the opposite way.

My favourite settlement is a warm, sunny spot on the windowsill, where I dream about the forthcoming day and also the past. I have absolutely no conscience about idleness, and no one expects work or activity. They find my laziness attractive and run their hands along my back in approval. Although I have a solitary nature, I like to spend time with my family. Playing games with the little black flies, or watching the cautious appearance of the light beige mouse who peers from its home in the cupboard. When friends appear, I land with a soft thud at their feet, and rub myself from nose to tail around their ankles. My increasing contentment becomes obvious. I lick myself and purr.

Alan Creith (14)

My Pedigree Suffolk Ewe-lamb

I purchased this ewe-lamb in Ballymoney market. This was on the 10th of September 1984. It was the first pedigree sale which was held in Ballymoney market and proved to be very interesting and also very valuable. All the sheep were judged in the morning at 9 a.m. and the sale was due to commence at 11.30 a.m. I had to play rugby that morning so I asked my father if he would go into the sale and buy me a ewe-lamb if I wasn't back on time. Luckily I was back on time for the sale. I went into the ring stand and it was packed but I eventually found my father. I told him that I was going out to have a look at the ewe-lambs. When I went out I was so impressed with all the ewe-lambs that I wanted to buy them all. This I knew I couldn't do as I only had the money for one of them. I made my pick after some very hard deciding. My pick was lot number 98. After the ram-lambs had been sold the ewe-lambs were due to come in. The first one was lot number 81. It made 123 guineas.

I thought to myself that they wouldn't need to get much higher or I wouldn't be able to buy any of them. It came to lot number 97 and I was becoming excited. In walked number 98. I didn't start the bidding but it started at 103. I bid against three men and I made sure I became the owner of lot number 98. I bid to 125 guineas which is £131.25. It was a large price to pay but I wanted to start off with good quality stock. When my father heard I had bought it he was amazed that I bought such an expensive animal.

When I got it home, I turned it straight into the field with the ram. I watched it very carefully to see when it would tup. Unfortunately it didn't tup until the 16th of November as it was very young.

This year for the first time we got our ewes scanned to see how many lambs they were carrying. When it came to mine, I watched with great care and the man said she had two lambs in her. I was greatly amazed as it is not a usual thing for ewe-lambs to carry two lambs.

I know that these lambs will not be born untill the middle of April of this year. I hope that when they are born that they will be healthy and strong lambs.

The other night, I was wondering how I could get the pedigree of this ewe-lamb so I decided to telephone Mr R.A. McClinton of Ballymena who was the previous owner of this ewe-lamb. When I started to tell him all about her he said that the pedigree of her was A4/X21. He seemed a very nice man and he told me all the details of how the pedigrees worked. He ended up by suggesting that he would get me a form to fill in my pedigrees on and also he would send me the Pedigree Suffolk Society's Annual for 1984. I am still waiting for this information to come through the post.

Christopher Beattie (12)

I hope to become a member of the Pedigree Suffolk Society of N. Ireland but to achieve that you have to own at least five pedigree suffolk ewes. I hope to build up to this through the years to come. There is a lot of hard work involved in it. I spend about three quarters of an hour every night feeding and caring for all the sheep on our farm.

When it comes to June all the sheep have to be sheared and this is a very hard job. When I establish myself in the pedigree business I shall have to spend many hours grooming and shearing my sheep for shows and sales. All the pedigrees that you will come across will have their backs cut flat to make them look broad. They also will have their hindquarters fluffed out to make them look broad. Whenever you are buying sheep you have to watch and make sure you run your hand over their backs and hindquarters and then you see for real how broad they are. It is very deceiving when they are groomed because they look broad to your eye but to touch they are not quite so broad.

My ewe-lamb is doing extremely well and I hope she is the start to a good career of pedigree suffolks for many years to come in my business.

Keith Guthrie (11)
Clitter, Clatter

Clitter, clatter, bib on
Honor Oak Estate
Noise, Noise everywhere.
People shouting.
The butcher shouts come back,
you silly dog.
You just stole my sausages.
Neighbour's music in the night.
What a horrible life on the Honor Oak
Estate.
Our little baby wakes up at night.
So we are moving to Milton Keynes.
Moving to Milton Keynes, Thank God
and my dad.

'Ex-Beatles in Seance' by Steve Baily

Last night, December the 8th, 1984
    It is reported that the <u>Ex-Beatles</u>
    Namely George Harrison,
Ringo Starr
    and
    Paul
        McCartney `
Met up with Yoko
    Ono,
        wife of the
        Deceased
SINGER, John
Lennon.

An A-Registration
(A-Registration)

    Two-Tone

    Rolls
    Royce
arrived at the
<u>EXCLUSIVE HILTON HOTEL</u>

IN
Park
    Lane

An. . . Informant   <u>RANG</u>
    THE. . .
 SUNDAY MIRROR

Stat-
ing that the car would
                (soon)

Bring the Af-
orementioned Persons
to
the ho-
Tel   the

DRIVER
said To

(Reporters)

'I can't
say whether I'll

be
Bringing the

BEATLES

or
not.

I can't say y-
es or
No
(to anything).'

The CAR
returned later
carrying a

Woman thought to
Be

YOKO ONO

the

SUNDAY MIRROR
photographer   Mike

Davies

said

'I'm *95* per cent
Sure it   Was her'

Some sources have
              sug-

          gested
          that

                    THE
                              BEATLES

              were attempting

              A SEANCE

(as it is the fourth anniversary of john

                              Lennon's   ...   DEATH
)   .

    at one point the driver was seen to carry through some
hand luggage   .

          'Ouija Bo-
          ards?'

                    (i wonder if they
                    simply might be
                         there to
                         mourn
                         his

                    untimely

                    death

                         ?

)

Highway 61 Revisited

She dreamt.

Dreamt of having normal eyes, a voice, and no hateful, loathsome Ultra-sight, the extra eye of far-seeing. Her brother, Peetra of the kill-stick, he did amer her. In that way, glad was she, glad she had the MindSpeak, and glad too that only Peetra was open to her secret tongue. Because though she was feared, even Non-amered now, if she so much as touched another mind, she would be cast out, and her strange octacles seccered away.

Sol cut the sky, awakening her. It glinted off her golden octacles: octacles without pupil or iris, just simple, glowing gold. She reached out tendrils of thought groping.

'Oh my brother Peetra of the kill-stick, do you sleep?'

'Oh my sister Alzabeph of the gold octacles, I sleep not, did your sleep-cycle pass with peace?'

'Oh brother my sleep-cycle passed without event as normal and without a scare-dream, did you have a peace-night or were scare-dreams unto you?'

'My sleep-cycle was a peace-night I thank you, oh my sister, I rise now.'

She closed. Upon rising she looked at her pale, naked body, and sighed. Dressing, she thought, if the kill-stick was not I would not be here o they hate and fear me why why why?

The entrance to her casser was swept aside. She whirled round, gasping, but it was her brother. They hugged wunanuther.

'Bonmorn, my sister. Sol has rose, and my B'letts are problaty complete. I go now to Fredrig the blag smerth. Do you desire to companise me?'

'Oh my brother I do not know. . . '

'Fear not, sister mine. Jests and prencks contra you, I will ward off, and a thrown mizzle will not penetrate your far-sight. Companise me, serraplay?'

'If 'tis your wish my brother.'

''Tis my wish, oh sister, come.'

They stepped out into the humid air and propered to Fredrigs smerthy. They could hear his hamm'r beating against the iyorn. As they ambuled along the ancient nigrer via, they passed near a group of people, Jesting and riddicling. As they went among the turb, a man muttered, 'Begone, mutabitch, your kind of filth should dwell in the shit where you were spawned!'

Peetra's zord was out of its scab'rurd as the verbs were uttered. The life of the mascule lay in the temper of a young warrer.

'Insult again sister or late mother mine, Foulsod, and I seccrate your gizzard shall.' The verbs came in a base growl from Peetra's thrax.

'Your pardoning, I orra indeed. Your sister is her own fem.'

The zord was sheathed. Even at dorry-quatrer, Peetra was one of the Harwar-Sixchyun's best warrers, especialty since he had found the kill-stick in the wreckag of a Wartanck. He had errerd in the silvest, searching for game, when he had come accross an old Wartanck, its great kill-stick pointed to the Elyzians. The place held great forebodeing for him, and he was inclined to proper away, but curiosness pushed him towards the Death-Vessel. Inside, were dorr charred and decaying corr'pzes. He was just to proper, when he vidded a Novi object in a pile of burnt papyrer. He had picked it up and vidded it was a longe tube with a handle, and paucy leev'r at yoon end, and also another tube atop the magner yoon, with glazz lenzes. He vidded through them and realised they biggified things. Suddenly there was a 'blang!' and a flazash of light, and the handle drived backtowards into his thrax. He viddiplussed at it in incredible. He picked it up, gingerful, and vidded it all over. Then he propered back to the villij.

Since then, he had intelged how it proplelled paucy mizzles, called 'B'letts', and how to constract them. He had told the Blagsmerth how to constract them, the B'letts, and collected some novi ones every sizday. As he did hoday, on the quatry nonth of sunner.

'Bonmorn, Fredrig,'

'Aaaah, Bonmorn, Bonmorn indeed Peetra. An Bonmorn to you, Alzabeph!'

Alzabeph smiled. In the whole sicky villij, she dellected Fredrig, even amered him, for he did not hate her. Once, she had in the silvest, and, other than Peetra, he alone had goned to sherch for her. And he had found her.

'Be the B'letts parrered, Fredrig?'

'Yeay, up all the sleep-cycle I was, parerring them!' he said, in Mocke Rue, 'Take them! I am done with B'letts!'

'Aaaah, you're an amico, Fredrig.'

'That I know! I be perfection itself!' He roared with laughter. 'And,' he said in a softer tone,'I have something for you, O Alzabeph.' He held out to her a amerly, paucy silpha ring, set with couloured glazz. She was very touched, and glowing tears drippled down her cheeks. She looked at the ring and putted it on her indacs finger. She hugged Fredrig.

'Ooo, found a ald lad'l by the poowel. Meltened it down, to make a brazilett for Elan, then found a paucy bit left over,' he explained, 'and the gryn glazz was from an old boott'l I found.'

'Anyway, here's the B'letts.' He handed Peetra a small wooded bok, frull of paucy B'letts. 'Take caution!' he added. 'The small rooj mark on a paucy lot, indicates a novi idea of me. I hollowed, and filled them with sticleback poisent! A graze will cause Mort!'

'This is an idea indeed! Very novi. Bon, Bon! Gratias, gratias!' said Peetra in wonder. He filled the kill-stick with a poisent B'lett.

'Bon bye, Fredrig, and gratias again.' They turned, and begunned the ambler back.

'My sister, I need to proper on a hunt in silvest, for meat. I shall be returned presently.'

'Bon O brother here shall I wait.'

She went to her casser, holding all the time, mai soon he passed beyond her range. She sat on a cheyr, and began to write a poem. She had practised writing since she was paucy. She did it with a scratchy knibb on stiff papyrer.

☼ cycl was gon
☾ cycl was com
? Novi o-☾
Hold FOR ME

Her writing became blurred as she weepded. Suddenly a rough voice yelled, 'Get up, Mutabitch. Get up on your foul legs!' She vidded up in incrediblaty. A turb of angry mascules and fems, led by the mascule who had insulted her earlier. He grabbed her brown hair and yankded her up. 'Get up, I said!' She opened her mouth in pain. He threw her into the turb where dorr more mascules grabbed and threr her into the via. She got up and tried in vain to proper but they grabbed and holded her. The premier mascule grabbed her shift, and ripped it down the midian, so it fell straight down. She gasped and tried to pull her rukers about her, but the mascules held her. The mascule grabbed her, and while the other dorr held her, he beat her with a knotted rope, then approached her with mort in his octacles and was about to entrer her when she, in despratation threw her mind around.

Altheworld flinched involuntarily, but one mascule, in another part of the villij, vidded up from his work, grabbed a novily forged zord and ran off. He did not intellge why.

A roar of rage shook the Turb.

Lyndan Brewer (12)

'No!' Fredrig smashed through, 'No! Not that a masculine warrer, of the Harwar-Sixchyun, could attack,' his octacles strayed to the red weals across her corr'pz, 'and, and beat and ravage a defencless fem? I SAY NO!'

With rage and power oozing from his every pore, he swung the zord. Fredrig was a plusmuscular mascule, with his work, and with additional rage-power, the zord swung down and with a noise like a spade in wet turf, it bit the kneck, crated the spinalerl column, and passed through to the other side. The head of her attacker rolled off Alzabeph, and the mort octacles viddiplused at her in accusation. The bllod oozed sluggishly from the kneck, dien suddenly fountained forth, covering her in rooj fluid.

'Go, fem. Quickly! Into the silvest! Get a zord and protectashield from my forj. I join you shall soon!'

She propered. As she did so, she heard sounds of battle from the square. She entered Fredrig's place, grabbed the nearest zord and protectashield, and propered.

Peetra comed back deoectedly. A mal trip. Nothing, mai. . . what was that?

'Peetra! I help need!' He heard Fredrig's voice, and the clashing of metal meeting metal. He propered, cocking his killstick.

'Haar!' A Blang echoed in the air and yoon of the attackers fell mort.

'I come, Fredrig!'

'Non, fool, proper! Your sister is endangered!'

'What?'

'The foulsods attacked her! She propered to the silvest.'

'Come, dien!'

With a last slash they propered down the via to the silvest, grabbing protectashields from Fredrig's forj.

She propered. Thorns ripped across her Newd corr'pz, drawing more bllod adding the now solidificating on her. With a start, saw a plant ahead. With thorns as well, but these waved invitingly, with no breeze! She knew this was a mutobramble. Yoon scratch, and all the network of stems would imprison her, drawing vital body salts with their thorns.

She turned, and whimpered with sick fear. Voices approached. She crouched down and listened.

'Cheer up, amico. We will find her soon!'

'Oh no please.'

'But Fredrig, we've sherched for yorncks, and no. . . '

With a sob and blast of intelliging, she leaped in front of her brother.

They ambuled, as they had done for the whole sol-cycle, it seemded. . .

'O brother, do you receive the noise of burdds?'

'Yes, sister.'

'She talks, does she?' Since they had told him, Fredrig could not get over her MindSpeak.

'It is a sound to make yoon glad.'

'It is. But do not let any pack you.' Suddenly a squirrel darted in front of them. They backed away nervously.

'Haa. . . I see. . . Muta. . . Gold eye. . . help me. . . ' the squirrel stammered.

'Whaat?' she thought. 'How does it know. . ?'

Peetra raised the kill-stick and the squirrel scuttled off.

'It came too close. Mort unto you those tall'ns give.'

Later in the eve they came to a starg, evil horns glinting in the lunalight, 'Hhhu, Nnnooo kkihlll mmmere I yooo ammiiiccooo. . .' and Peetra shot him.

'Good eating for us, catiousness take though. The venn'm sac lie beneath the prongs.' They made flame, and enrosted the corr'pz.

'I had a novi idea!' said Fredrig. He milked the venn'm sacs, and let the light bleur liquid dripple over their zords.

''Tis baneful,' he said grimly, 'but the need is ours.'

That night, they took turns to sentinard. As Peetra did so, he heard a paucy russle. He rose, speedily.

'Who beeth there? Who?' he demanded angerfully. Another russle answered him.

'Who is there?' he yelled.

'Nyaar, killl. . . !' a hoarse voice screamed, and quatrey vulv'vreens leaped into sight. Their tales swished and thrumped the ground, menacingly. 'Mmeeeeaaatt!' said yoon. 'Gruun. . . Hungggerrful!' screamed the same yoon. They all holded clubbers in their forepands. They advanced.

With a yell, yoon attacked Alzabeph. She dodged, and full of savaery, sheathed her zord in the beestee, then gasped with horror. The blood stained her zord. The vulv'vreen choked as the starg venn'm took effect. The others were not so luckful. The last thing Alzabeph vidded before the clubber hit the back of her kneck, was Fredrig and Peetra falling. Then the sleep of nonconshusfullness hit her.

The premier thing that Peetra vidded as he woke, was the kindly looking old mascule beinding over him concernfully.

'Ah. Awake. Yes.' The mascule nodded his head wisenessfully. 'No. Don't move. Too tired. Tough fight. Yes.'

'Who. . . ?'

'Philipson. James B. At. . . erm. . . your service, Sir!' The masculer tongue was novi, with novi verbs, and strange pauses. But it was understandable. 'Ah. One moment. Yes. Friends. Your Friends wake.' And he approached the other dorr, lying some distance away. Peetra saw he was in a plus large casser. But their host was speaking:

'Now. Yes. Hello. I am James Philipson. I am your friend. Or amico. As you say. You, I suppose, are wondering how you are. . . here. Yes?' They murmered assent.

'Yes. I also, erm, have. A gun, yes. I have one. And the were wolves are. . . dead. Yes. But now. Important. Who are. . . you?' he asked. He looked at Alzabeph, who shook her head helplessly.

'She no voice has. Radioness clogs her tongue,' explained Peetra.

'Ah. Yes. Of course, a mutant.' His voice softened, 'Poor girl.'

'We are of the warrer tribe, the Harwar-sixchyun. . . '

'That will do. Tell me, is there a road in your village?'

'R-road?'

'I mean, via?'

'Yes. A nigrer yoon, with a blanch line dividing it.'

'Ah. . . I see. Do you know where the name Harwar-sixchyun comes from?'

'No.'

'Ah. Well. Many years ago, the world was full of people. Powerful people. With fantastic engines, music, and a magical life source, called Elektrersiti. With this power, they could do almost anything. But. They made another power. Called Nyookliah power. Stronger that Elektrersiti. But more deadly. With an evil effect, and side-power, called Radioactervisness, which warped, and killed people. They made big bombs, which are like huge bullets, which burst, over big places. These bombs were full of Radioactervisness. "Defence". Now. At that time, the world was split up. Into big countries. .Where we are, was called Ham'riga. We were ruled by an Evil sorcerer, called Ronaltarraycun. He had one big enemy called "The Red Warriors of the Sorfiet Unified". They were led by Shrerninkhof. Ronaltarraycun had a bad woman as an allie from across the water, from the isles of Brittaly. She was known as the "woman of iron". But her true name was Murgisfatshur. One day the two evil sorcerers ganged against the valiant red warriors. They threw big bombs. So the red warriors threw them back. They ruined the Earth.

'That was a thousand years ago. We have lost civilisation. But I cling to it. My name you see. From a true civilised name. Oh, and of names. . . the "Harwar-Sixchyun" comes from this. In those days, they had magic riding things, of iron and steel, called "automobiles". These ran on big vias called roads. The bigger roads were called "Highways" and these were numbered. You, Peter. Count to ten. . . sorry, dizz.'

'Yoon, dorr, trey, quatry, sank, siz, set, och, non, dizz.'

'You see. The tongue has been perveted. Anyway. Back then, they said "Sizzy-yoon", as "Sixty-one", and used it as foundations for the village. And you, my dear Alzabeph. Ah,' his voice was soft, 'Yes. You see, today, still, there are bomb remnants, occasionally, radioactervisness finds its way to a mother's womb, and does its evil deed. You are a victim. But do not fear. I think. . . you will prevail.' He turned to address them all.

'But now. I have something.serious to say. I have searched for such followers. You shall do great work!'

All could sense that he was excited about something. He leaned forward eagerful.

'You. . .' A sigiter whistled through an open freetrer. 'Hhnaaa . . .' He made an Evil sound as the styel tipped cap't penetred his Luvorgan, ceasing the neverstop pumping.

Fredrig and Peetra grabbed their zords. Alzabeph hesited. Since the vulv'reen died at her rukers, she had been sick at the thought. More Mort, she stand could not. . . .

But it vidded as though she would be spared. Instead of ripping and secrating for meat, the vulv'reens rushed away. . . Gleenessfully.

'Appears it not, amicae, he was the target of their evil? Aaah, but life is sweet, it takes mort to realise how plus so,' stated Fredrig, mournessly.

'But we should get on,' said Peetra, 'Sleep-cycle approaches.'

They stepped onto the road.

As they approached the setting sol, the last lines of her unfinished poem ran through Alzabeph's mind:

'Sol-cycle has gone.
Sleep-cycle has come.
What will new day hold for me?
Whateverso beit,
Bon or non,
I will accept it, Joyfully. . . . '

Lyndan Brewer (12)

MELANCHOLY THOUGHTS

Kirstin Cox (10)

Kirstin Cox (10)
Tea-Time

I sit by the fire with my chips and beef,
My peas and gravy and lemonade,
My ice-cream and poured hot chocolate.
 – And there in the TV sits a child,
staring out at my dinner and me,
Staring and dying, wasting away.
In our living room.
Its flat body is sticks of bone and skin.
Flies are buzzing round its head,
Death-bringers to its scaled face.
A baby cries out for its mother's milk.
I am full. I sip warm milk from my cup.
And think of all the food in our cupboard,
All the meat that we eat in a week.
I wish that crying child
Could wet its mouth with milk,
Feel warm at night in a cot and blankets.
They say we've mountains of grain,
Lakes and lakes of milk
Yet my stomach's full, while his is hollow.
And I live as he dies.
He dies as I live.

Why? Why?

The Conquerors

Day 105. The 'real' date, however, escapes me and I've lost all track of time. What I do know is that the inevitable erupted exactly one hundred and five days ago. I look around the small Harrier F-15, observing that here I could imagine things were back to normal – that I was flying my plane over my city, Winnipeg, and marvelling at the magnificent stability of the skyscrapers and the minuteness of the matchbox cars. Alas, I was reluctantly awoken from my dream, after being nudged by my companion, or should I say convictor? Mr Chyme. . . . There was a time when I would wistfully look up at Mr Chyme's office hoping that one day I would be able to meet him or even converse with him, but in reality I knew the dream of promotion to the 'important place' from being the insignificant council member of Winnipeg State was just a vision. The superior ruler of the United States would never have the time. . . . Now, both of us had all the time in the world – but we were dumb. The prospect of witnessing 'my' unforgivable doing (I relentlessly, and perhaps wrongly, blamed all action onto myself because I was one of the three million majority of politicians who had voted for 'continuation of the arms race') was unthinkable, yet I was nearly there.

'Landing soon, sir,' murmured the pilot, his face haggard, looking thirty years older than he was. 'Moscow coming into view.'

'Okay, boy,' drawled the President (Of what, I wondered?), 'we're ready,' glancing towards me. I looked away, wishing that I had not been one of the healthiest (and one of the living) so to have the 'pleasure' of flying with the beloved Mr Chyme, to see Russia for ourselves and the decay we together had set forth.

The Harrier landed jerkily and jolted to an abrupt stop. I started shaking unconsciously, as if with fever, and I could feel a cold sweat creeping up the back of my neck. 'Help me God,' I whispered, even though I had vowed never to pray again.

'Right, Perry, let's go.'

'Yes, sir,' I said softly.

'I'll wait here,' whispered the pilot, croakingly, obviously seen all he wanted.

The President stepped out cautiously, shielding his eyes from the orange light of the sun-down. I following, knees feeling like the sound waves of the rare warbler, entering a world of discoloured earth with apprehension and disgust, the only object faintly familiar to my old world being the sun, even that shining uncommonly bright. I breathed in the still stale air, taking in the stench of rot and (dare I say it?) death.

'Let's go and investigate over there,' said Mr Chyme as if shouting, even though he was barely whispering.

'There's some buildings,' he added, pointing out what appeared to be a huge rubbish dump. I stared disbelievingly at the President because of the totally unaffected manner in which he spoke, physically and mentally. It was as if he was an adventurous child who had discovered a good tree to climb. I wanted to spit in his face, then decided to save the little energy remaining in me to follow him.

BY SUNDOWN WE CAME TO THE HIDDEN
VILLAGE WHERE ALL THE AIR WAS STILL

The village was indeed hidden, a few leafless scorched trees, faintly resembling a wood, stood as if bewildered but not losing their dignity, holding up the lead-like branches like the starving reach to beg. The deafening silence we held for the dead.

AND NO SOUND MET OUR EARS, SAVE
FOR THE SORRY DRIP OF BLACKENED TREES

'Which way now?' I asked, and then added sarcastically, 'Mr President.'

'Through the gate, boy,' he replied, ignoring my rude comment. I followed him yet again cringing at the screeching sound of rusty hinges, sounding like my soul – crying. We walked, on what we guessed was the remains of the 'High Street', the buildings being just heaps of rubbish, grit, dust and other debris, with occasional gusts of air banging round broken houses as if looking for the door.

'Look there!' I shouted, 'a bird,' I ran quickly to a cracked window, where a budgerigar was in an old red cage, pressing its body against it, as if trying to escape. Its beak was wide open. 'It wants food,' I laughed, joyful at the sight of life apart from us.

'No. . .' murmured Mr Chyme, but I didn't hear. Instead, I opened the cage, not noticing his protests, and almost screamed when the stiff, dummy-like body fell onto the hard surface.

'Oh, God,' I gasped (the previous happiness draining from my face), and covered my eyes. The President walked over to me and gently pulled me out of the frozen position I had curled into, 'Come on, son,' he soothed but with a slight shake to his voice. 'Let's go on.'

A DEAD BIRD IN A RUSTING CAGE, STILL
PRESSING HIS THIN TATTERED BREAST AGAINST
THE BARS, HIS BEAK WIDE OPEN.

I sniffled and wiped my tears away with a dirty blood-stained handkerchief.

We hurried on now, desperate to return to the normality of the aeroplane. Unfortunately another shock hit us: a rustling from underneath a pile of bricks protruded the uneven road. We both froze in our tracks. I could feel the same burning sensation, my stomach turning inside out and a choking lump rapidly developing at my throat. At first I thought it was a cat, but later realised it was the remaining part of a starved dog – a mongrel. It probably was a stray alley before (what other dog would've survived!), its fur virtually non-existent apart from a few patches covering the prominent ribs. Its legs thin as pencils broken in more than one place, caused it to limp to the trees, maybe to its cemetery. Now, even Mr Chyme was crying, the first emotions I had ever known him to display, the silent tears trickling down his cheek and dripping off the stubbly chin, one by one as if committing suicide.

AS WE HURRIED THROUGH THE WEED-GROWN
STREET, A GAUNT DOG STARTED UP FROM
SOME DARK PLACE AND SHAMBLED OFF ON
LEGS AS THIN AS STICKS INTO THE WOOD,
AT LEAST TO DIE IN PEACE.

The heaps of rubble thinned towards the end of the street, so we turned a corner and set off back, my mind filled with immense grief that led to physical fatigue as well. Suddenly, Mr Chyme stopped still for a minute, his eyes averted to one place at the right of us. I turned, puzzled for a second only that seemed like hours of intense observation. The second was enough to see that morbid sight: a stiff broken body sprawled before the shattered door, of a young girl, her frock grey with faint marks of yellow flowers. It was obvious she had been a survivor as her face or body wasn't burnt or scarred anywhere, her hair unsinged – she had starved to death and, like the dog, her leg and rib-bones could easily have been counted. My stomach flipped and I vomited blood, which I felt was from my heart, pierced by the accusative gaze from her cold dark eyes; 'It's your fault,' they seemed to say.

NO ONE TOLD US VICTORY WAS LIKE THIS; NOT
ONE OF US WOULD HAVE EATEN BREAD BEFORE
HE'D FILLED THE MOUTH OF THE MEAGRE CHILD
THAT SPRAWLED STIFF AS STONE BEFORE THE
SHATTERED DOOR.

'She looks like my daughter,' cried Mr Chyme, his whole being shivering violently as I hugged him and led him to the Harrier.

'I pressed the button for all this to happen,' he groaned disbelievingly.

'Yes, you did, you bastard,' I thought for a moment, wanting to strangle him. Instead I repeated, 'Come, it's done now, let's go home.'

'Home?' he said, his voice overwhelmed with an almost pathetic sadness. I knew there was no home, not here, there, not anywhere.

THERE WAS NOT ONE OF US WHO DID NOT
THINK OF HOME.

The lines in capitals are taken from Henry Treece's poem 'The Conquerors' and are reproduced by permission of John Johnson, literary agents.

Charles Mawer (16)

Potato Blight

A body lies in Ballymena, an ode to
persecutors' piety,
His monkey eyes blindly focus on the
Battle of the
Boyne. His ears are deaf to the

Fenian call, his nose rejects the stench
of rotten potatoes,
and his kneecaps bear the scars of a
turncoat's treachery.
He lies motionless in the green, green

super grass and dreams of Sundays and the
Boy's Brigade.
Easter remembrance, Christ's rising,
Easter rising, Christ forgotten.
Public school children learn the present tense

of Morior. As Hector stalks the blood-grey
Dublin backstreets,
teenage troops play soldiers in their petrol bombing
hatred nurturing undergrowth.
Mars their god of war slips chocolate crumbly from

their blood-stained lips. Styx and stones
won't break their bones,
riot shields won't hurt them. Achilles brought
to heel
by their armalited glare. De Valera glares

Big Brother style, from each and every
madman's eye.
UDR, the Ultimate Death Role for
countless corpseless
souls, who lie in united Ireland's

state. Posthumous, knowing poets whose
cry for mercy
goes unheard. Hunger stricken patriots
suck their
orange-coloured rosettes and dream of

emerald skies. Propaganda's shrapnel booms from
megaphones' muzzles,
Pulpits reverberate from the same, insane
hellfired preachers.
Paisley points the poisoned finger and witchdoctors

execute in style. Revolutionaries practise
preventive medicine,
it's they who need proscription for their ever
darkening tumours.
Armagh who art in heaven, hellhole

be thy name. Siegfried Sassoon stands proudly
with the dead
'so forsaken and still', the tidal wave of blood
floods Shannons shores
and the gore rises gurgling from the bogs of

Londonderry. Cromwellian memories stoke
Sinn Fein's pyre,
Drogheda burns like a seventeenth century
valkyrie,
united with Wexford in their marriage of

malcontent. Progressive society's
aggressive answer
stings the moralists' hearts as they sip
their whisky and Sodom,
and all the while the stench of rotten

potatoes. I bring you tales of a banana republic
to shock the portals
of your aristocratic homes, to shock your
golf clubbing,
vicious social circle, where the only

charity is an opposite to the
widow's mite.
But I can't be talking about you.
You're not like that.
I'm talking about someone else,

Surely I'm talking about someone else
or am I?
If I shock do not over worry or
you may strain
Your Harley Streeted features in an ever so

ugly frown. That's better, look on the bright side
of life,
Or is that somehow wrong? No matter.
As your tragic empire,
falls and another piece of red leaves

Stanley's stamp album, put your slippered
feet up,
And think no longer of my heinous tale
but light your pipe
and smell no more that rotten stench. . . .

James Egan (16)
It's the Same God

In the streets,
Grime, dirt and fear in children's faces –
a shining example of remorse and reconciliation.
Barbed wire and broken glass proclaim
Our unbounding love for one another.

In the streets,
Khaki camouflaged combat jackets seem
a strange sort of ecumenism.
It's hard to turn the other cheek –
when you're dead.

The sun won't come out today –
Take our love and mark it down as surplus.

In the church (which one?),
Chained to our respective fury dousing pews,
Handcuffed to pig-eared Testaments;
we are spiritually enlightened.

In the church,
Does Agnus Dei seem a fitting war cry?
Are purple vestments suitable battle gear?
Will peace ever be found in our
torn and shattered land?

It's the same God you know but –
which side is He on?

Sean Kenny (16)

Guy Burt (12)
In the Dock

The Trial of Tomorrow

Witness for the Prosecution

JUDGE.   Call Despair.

DESPAIR. My Lord, you must surely understand that this
              Tomorrow is but a
            figment of the imagination,
            an illusion, nay, a delusion
            on which the souls of weak worms feast
            but grow no fatter, and starve, and die,
            That tepid mass in one's stomach
            when reality breaks, as a wave,
            and you know, yes my lord, you know
            that despite all your strivings
            you cannot change the world in which you live.
            Therefore surely Tomorrow is cause for worry,
            cause for uncertainty,
            cause for jealousy?
            Cause, no less, for misgivings, for useless
                preparations,
            cause even for Hope?
            And for the belief that tomorrow brings more and
            better than today?
            All the trees bear fair fruit tomorrow,
            But in reality – they are bitter.
            Great flowers bloom tomorrow –
            But in reality, they wither.
            My lord, I rest my case.

JUDGE.   Call Typical.

TYPICAL. My Lord, I represent all the ordinary thousands.
            My case is one of false pretences,
            of an inexplicable urge not to differ,
            Not to break new ground,
            but to tread the same mill until we drop.
            My witnesses are smog, old warehouses

now abandoned, and patched with plastic,
And the knowledge that day after day
Is the same.
If a life consists, M'Lud, of days alike,
then surely Tomorrow is no novelty?
Tomorrow must give way to Today.
My Lord, I rest my case.

JUDGE. Witness for the prosecution, do you call any more
speakers?

WFTP. But one, M'Lud. Call Reality.

REALITY. My Lord, the populace is under the impression
that all one's worries will vanish
should one but wait.
This, My Lord, is untrue.
Left unattended, worrying matters grow
as a canker. Surely then,
with the abolition of Tomorrow
All these aspects will be attended to today?
My Lord, look around you. See the threats,
Pollution, the slow death of the environment
That increase tomorrow?
See the extinction of species, the imminent danger
of Nuclear War, that could break out tomorrow?
That tomorrow, we may be no more?
My Lord, I rest my case.

Witness for the Defence

JUDGE. Call Tomorrow.

CLERK. Absent, M'Lud. The trial is to be conducted in his
absence.

WFTD. Call Hope.

HOPE. Gentlemen of the jury, Tomorrow is wonderful.
Sometimes there is the happy knowledge that
Tomorrow is a day of rest.
Sometimes you may have Tomorrow to finish
that which you have begun.

Tomorrow is a day to start anew, to start afresh.
To forget what is done today and just to live.
Tomorrow is a comfort, a refuge.
'It will all be all right tomorrow,' people say,
and they are right.
For what, M'Lud, could be worse than today?
Tomorrow is for seeing flowers, for hearing birds,
For not caring, for loving.
Tomorrow is an aid to help us through now.
We all need Tomorrow.
M'Lud, I rest my case.

JUDGE.   Are there any more witnesses for the defence?

WFTD.   Only Hope, My Lord. Only Hope.

JUDGE.   Then let the jury consider their verdict.

Ralph Wood (8)
Tombstones

Tombstones lean to a side.
I was sitting by Loise Curry and Harry Walters' grave.
There I sit.
Weathered graves crumble.
A mottled blotch of granite.
Lies in hard soil.
As flowers blow,
The two bodies lie in peace.
In the earth's dead prison.
Lichens peel off the grave.
A pitted, etched wooden grave,
Stands sorrowfully,
Cracked beside the new splendoured grave
The wind blows.
In silence
A jagged tree waves in the wind.
The scabs on the tombstone look ugly.

Clare Milner (15)

The Escapologist

They buried him under twelve tons of concrete.
It was quick setting.
They estimated that the sheer weight of the concrete would
crush his coffin-prison.
Chained in a plastic cell with no way out.
Was this to be his last
Attempt to defy the laws of nature and humanity?
'Pour the concrete!'
They gave him approximately three minutes to live,
Three minutes to escape.
Would the bonds of steel and stone defeat the new Houdini?
One minute passes.
They glance nervously at digital watches on executive wrists.
Two minutes pass.
There is no movement from the entombed life, no ripple
In the concrete.
Houdini himself nearly died in an attempt to escape from
A trial burial.
He seems to preside over this event, slowing down time, but
The third minute passes.
There is a murmur, they begin to notice the tombstone already
In place at the graveside.
It seems that this is indeed to be the final escape.
A finger, wait, a hand
Rises from the grave, attached to an arm, a shoulder,
His head reaches the surface.
As they cheer, the man struggles out of the twelve foot
Prison. His grey eyes
See nothing. they are blind, plugged with concrete. His ears
Are grey and deaf.
His grey hair matches his grey hands, grey face, grey body.
He stands, staggers,
Falls to his knees in gratitude. He is a survivor.
He lives to die.
This man has proved that it is possible to escape anything,
Even death.

SEASONAL THOUGHTS

Emma Rothero (12)

Nicola Eastwood (14)

At the Races

Voluptuous pink bows
adorn the pampered hats,
Vying with each other
like a subdued carnival.
Smoked salmon sandwiches,
Caviar, Champagne,
Background the capering jockey colours,
Mounted on sinewed frames
of muscle and flesh.
These are the actors on the stage,
set, and ready for their cue.

The frenzy escalates,
sweeps across the grandstand
Like a fire carried by wind,
and subsides into the distance
Riding the crowd as a surfer rides the waves.

Peter Smith (8)

The Sea

The sea is blue and going out
To its deep green depths.
And little fish swim out with it
Under its white white foam.
Sea gulls and sea eagles soar
Giving out tremendous cries.
Seaweed lying on pointed rocks
Out on the horizon boats go along
When the sea goes out it leaves behind
Lots of little treasures.

Andrew Shearstone-Walker (12)

The Test

Was it dead? It could be. The bee lay there motionless. I knelt down. It flew up. It flew up and towards the umpire. This match is just so boring. I just look out there and a mural of faces stare back at me. It's like going into a hall of mirrors and seeing yourself everywhere you look.

The red polished ball caught the bright yellow sun. I turned round.

'Oh, nothing as usual. Come on, ball, come this way for once. I never thought it would be so hot. The sky is a weird colour today. It's the sort of colour when it rains. My garden needs a good rain, it hasn't had rain on it for at least a week. I hope my wife's roses will survive the drought. She absolutely loves roses. Red ones, yellow ones, white ones, white, yes, I think white is my favourite. White as a snowstorm, white as a vapour trail coming from a plane. Planes and buses are all the same. Noisy, smelly and people being ill because of travel sickness through reading books. I've read so many books lately my eyes are all funny. Our Jimmy's been funny lately. Think he's got flu. I wonder if he'll be at school tomorrow. Don't like school. Hate school. Always have, always will do. Hate food. Hate school food. It's awful. Our phone is an awful green. This grass is an awful green. Don't like the shade. Ball's coming.'

I caught the red ball and throwing it felt the sensation of the ball being caught. 'Weird, never felt that before. Spot on target! I've hit the stumps. Listen, the crowd are clapping me. Sounds like a swarm of bees. I got stung once by a bee. Bees are horrible. Don't like bees. Hate bees.'

'Somebody out, it's Fintstone. Poor Fintstone. What's this? Out for a duck. Fintstone is out for a duck. One more to get out. Agh, whattt was that? Rain. Must run, get to shelter.'

A drop of rain went down my face. 'Oh, no, game will have to be played again. Cold. Put jumper on. Boring game will have to be played again.'

I slowly walked across the field watching the umbrellas go up. Hearing the clicks as they lock into place. 'Hate rain. Hate cricket. I suppose I will have to grin and bear it!'

Timothy Daukes (8)

Poor Old Guy (November 5th)

It is nine o'clock in the evening and I am shivering. All I wear is half a sock, and a bit of towel for a cloak. There is a cobweb on my nose, and in it struggles a tired cranefly. My head is a humble turnip, and my arms are flimsy cardboard and my glass eye is shining. The brown mountain has been lit and the red giant leaps from its earthy bed. The bats are screaming, or is it the gunpowder flying from the tin which has been shut for so long? The crescent is gleaming like a jewel in its cabinet – as the moon wanes my wax toes drip, and I am very near to tears. My last thought is I wish I was down on the grass playing with the infants.

Victoria Mitchell (7)

Driftwood

Natalie Barker (7)

Swirling whirling twirling
Twisted driftwood.
You look like an elephant.
I hear you trump wickedly
Crabs hide in your eyes
Gloomy jelly fish sting your ideas
Haunted starfish wiggle
Their feet around your trunk
Sharks gnaw at
Your scarred ears.
Your head is a coffin
For sand, seaweed and shells.

93

Peter Smith (8)

Snow

Soft feathery snow comes silently down
Showing up against the white washed moon
Dropping down to the great dark field
Dropping silently
Casting down ghostly shadows
Against the sinister glare of the moon.

Then morning came
And the robin woke
And twittered angrily
As if to say
How dare it snow
Without informing me.

Sophie Harris (12)

Winter

Winter is a slipsish season,
When sugarsnow on the ground goes plip
People skatterskate down the hill
And down the lane I wibble and slip.

The sugarsnow is made in icemen
The children swoo and slitherdrop
How storwindy and chilkoo it is
The children's hair is cold and wetmop.

The icicles hang like daggerknives
Warning people away from the roofslope
Old people see children skiddle on the icy sidepathment
And wonderpuzzle if they can cope.

Paul Cunningham (16)

Younger Times in the Snow

Watching the slow white silence fall
I picture days of absence from school
When the old long avenue was brightly silenced
And we felt the crumple beneath our feet
And for the first time tasted the snow
Which spiked the forehead and numbed the tongue,
When we sharply sucked in the cold air
And blew a veil which would turn into cloud.

Those nights we stepped out
Into strange amber darkness
To face the white fun like squeaking pups,
And aimed our quickly rounded snowballs
At the street-lamp,
To be warned by old complainers,
To return sly cheek,
And to laugh when Dad came out
And slipped angrily on his backside.

Laughing was a dangerous game to play
That night,
But the pain I recall is
From not using gloves
And swollen feet from the
Endless slide under brilliant stars
That brought dizziness as I shut my tired eyes
Before the flickering fire.

Those mornings I would
Tug my brother awake
So we could both look out at
The orchard together
Where the clawed trees were frozen into silence,
The only movement the water from the spring
Trickling beneath the ice,
Where footprints of birds
Had barely broken the snow.

But now the tiny ones are out and digging,
Hurling snowballs and sliding forever
Underneath the wild stars;
I know that their wonder
Will be as mine was.

Tim Gilbert (11)

Autumn's Harvest

Who ate the first blackberry?
I did, I ate the first blackberry,
Its flesh was sweet,
Like a glossy, purple clot.

Who picked the last apple?
I did, I picked the last apple,
Autumn's blood was in it,
Like a rose red globe.

Who ripened the golden corn?
The sun did, the sun ripened the corn,
It shone with a golden crackle,
A sign of harvest life.

Who made the plums go purple and plump?
Some red, some green,
As hard as a tight knot,
Big, dark burning ovals.

Who cracked the first hazelnut?
The small mouse-brown spheres,
Crunchy, with a lustful taste,
A real harvest treat.

When will the damsons fall from the tree?
Their stalks so thin, like a spider's spin,
The juice like thickened harvest wine,
Leaving stains upon the tongue.

Lucy Wilson (9)

Memories

There was excitement once,
But not now,
There was colour and warmth once,
But not now,
There was noise once,
But not now.

The excitement has gone,
The colour, the warmth and the noise,
The night was once exciting,
But there's just a cold grey misty morning now,
The ashes are lying neatly,
It's like a silent battle-field.

The rubble is lying there,
Firework cases nailed each to a plank of wood,
Napkins from hotdogs,
Foil from baked potatoes,
Sticks from the toffee apples,
And dead dull sparklers that children have thrown down in
    disgust,
And plastic cups that once held coffee to warm you inside.

The fireworks were once lighting the dark night,
There were girls screaming when the bangers went up and
    exploded,
And cries of delight at the Catherine wheels and the golden rain,
People yelling at the Roman candles saying
'There I told you there would be seven.'

But now I tell myself it is a vision,
It is two nights away now,
Soon everything will arrive,
But that will be next year.
Everything will come again,
But that will have to wait until next year.

John Windrim (15)

Sleeping In

No doubt she braved the wet city

Awaken
In a state of embryonic bravura
To the ultra-violent squeek
Of the LED.

Astride the steps
Watching the water melon
The fish-net elevator
Past the passion-red extinguisher.

She slipped within
She kissed me
Away I drifted, away. . . .
Brought to my senses by the new world

And the tornado in the plastic bag.

Signals

The telephone
And the dead second
When you sit
Frozen with fear.

Your disappointment
And your relief
Signals
From another planet.

Maestro

He heeds no slow motion

Deep tan with the pure jersey
The balls of his feet
Embrace the green grass
And the fingers twist

The ball falls forward in space
Its precious leather
Spins like the world spins

He had been touched by the hand of God
The power of God was within him
Flames would fly forth with every six
He smashed to blue heaven

Tonight the crowds will cry again
To the crack of the bat
For a split second

TELLING THE TALE

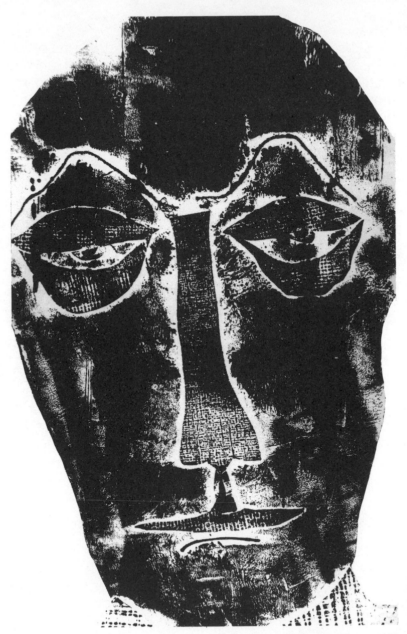

Emma Patey (12)

Jennifer Mcleish (15)

The Gift

Two men walked into our village one day, and the world ended. We did not know that they were to be the instruments of our doom because they looked like angels, not devils. Their skin was white as heat and they were dressed all in white like some messengers from the gods, although these clothes hid sticky black souls. But we did not know; how could we have known? They were strangers, and we treated them well.

It was a shimmering hazy day, the day the men came, and they stepped out of the jungle so bright in their whiteness that we were dazzled and came running from our huts to greet them. Old women and little children went up to touch their strange pure skin and we were all eager that they should rest and deliver their message from the gods. They seemed puzzled that we should request this and protested in a slow, faltering way of speaking with pauses to confer in some other tongue, that they were as human as ourselves. That was of course impossible, for their appearance was so different, but we believed their stories at the time.

They said that they had come from a distant land on the other side of a great lake, and were journeying in the jungle to spread the Word. They said this many times, and told our people that if they were treated well, given food and drink, and cared for, they would give our village a gift greater than we could imagine. They called this gift the Word, and told us that anyone who wanted could have it.

Fools! Fools that we were: like babies blinded by a momentary desire we asked them to give it to us, and the whole village came out to listen when they spoke of it daily. Knowing not that we were being enslaved by demons, everyone was anxious to have this gift of theirs.

The Word, the men said, had been spoken long ago by a god who was better than all the other gods, and he visited the earth disguised in human form to speak it. The Word was about how this one god had made the jungle and the river and the sky, and then made men to live there.

He wanted the men to be happy but they were wicked and would not be happy without killing other men, which made the big god sad. He decided to see for himself what it was like to be a man and disguised himself as a beggar, walking around and asking people to be kind. One day he saw a sick man, pretended to be a witch-doctor and cured the man by touching him as only the gods can do, but when the other people saw the healing they guessed that he was not a beggar and began to follow him around. They did not know that he was a god, and thought him to be perhaps a great chief of some tribe. He was happy that people were following him because it made them be good too.

But the real chief saw that it was not safe to have two chiefs in one tribe, and he ordered that the big god should be killed. He tied the big god to a tree to make him die, but of course the big god did not die; instead he flew up into the sky and disappeared.

Emma Quibell-Smith (15)

Suddenly everyone realised that he was the big god in disguise, and they were happy because he had shown that instead of dying and becoming ghosts, people would fly up into the sky and live up there. This was called the Word, said the two men, and it was the greatest gift that anyone could receive.

Some of us mentioned that we did not understand why the gift was so good, and they explained that we could not enjoy it until we forgot our old traditions and followed the big god. It was wrong to hold yearly sacrifices on the graves of our ancestors, wrong to pray to the sun to shine and the rain to fall, wrong to paint ourselves and dance as mankind has always done, wrong not to dress like the two men. This seemed like a lot to do in order to get the gift but we thought that we could easily dance again once we had it. How they talked and talked about the happiness which it would bring us, if only we would try to become like them in everything! They told us that the big god was coloured white like themselves, but that he was so big that he might even be kind to us, if we were very good. We wondered a lot about this big, white god, and one afternoon our witch-doctor asked them a question which had worried us all.

Did the big god make all the other gods, if he made everything?

The men thought for a while, spoke words we did not understand, and then told us that we were becoming such good, clean people since we had given up our savage ways that it was time to tell us something surprising.

There were no other gods.

How stupid we were not to have seen then that they were liars without a word of truth between them. Yet we believed even that, the biggest lie of all, because we were told that believing it was all part of the gift.

For a time, the two men were our teachers in everything, until the gods who we had deserted saw fit to strike down one of the liars with a mysterious disease that even our witch-doctor could not cure. They said that it was an affliction well-known in their own land, where it was called the pox, but only a mild case so the sufferer would recover within a week. We were overjoyed to learn our teacher would be well again, until he did recover and one of our people caught the disease. He did not get well; he died a slow, agonised death. When nine men of the village had

*Ruth
Silver (17)*

died and the false teachers professed not to understand it, we finally saw them for what they were.

All those lies about a big white god who was kind to his followers, when we who had listened to his teachings were being destroyed. Without further delay the village elders decreed that the two white men must be put to death as they had brought the sickness to our people. They were tied and burnt to death, and as we watched them, they themselves gave us the proof of the deception – they did not fly up into the sky as they had pretended.

Suddenly all was clear. The gods had allowed devils to come to us as a test of faith, to let them try to tempt us away from worshipping the true gods. We were ashamed, because we had failed the test and turned aside. At once we did penance by fasts and whippings and sacrifices, but we could not destroy the sickness, for it was our punishment. They had given us a gift; oh yes, among all the other lies that much was true. But the gift that they gave us was a deadly sickness, and the big white god was a lie.

Daniel Barker (11)

Odysseus and the Cyclops

The lonely Cyclops saw a winking ship ahead,
And smiled,
Then into his cave,
A bruise in the perfect cliff,
He ran.
A feast was prepared for his coming visitors;
To whom, when they arrived,
He showed every sign of hospitality
Until night fell.
He made a comfortable sleeping-place
For each of the newcomers,
And even let them swim in his basin;
But Odysseus, wicked as an atom-bomb,
Stayed up all night,
Discussing a devilish plan
To overthrow their host,
And rob him of his fine herbs and pure rubies.
At dawn, evil Odysseus and his men
Thrust a flaming stick,
As red as the stolen gems,
Into his eye.
In a moment of rage and killing pain,
One of his wildly thrashing feet
Crashed down onto his attackers,
As a ten-ton crate of lead,
Onto all but six of the pirates.
Next daybreak:
Odysseus and his men
Slithered out among the reeking sheep,
And made off in their battered ship,
With men and boat
Staggering under the weight of their loot,
Shouting insults as they sped away.
A different tale when they were home.

Short Story

The Dragon Slayer
Once, long, long ago, a very long time ago, about fifty centuries ago, there lived a boy called Jonathan. He lived in Germany.

They had a happy time playing in the parks, sunbathing, laughing and singing. One day a strange thing happened. In the middle of a hot summer day, it turned from lovely and light to pitch black. The air turned cold, winds blew and rain fell.

The children screamed and ran into their houses, closed the doors, and bolted the locks as a stream of fire shot through the sky.

The Gale
It was silent in the gale. Everyone was inside trembling, except for little Jonathan about seven years old. Oh, and wait a minute, here's the good news, he collects knives. He stood and watched, but he was not alone. One big fat bully was looking too. The fire came nearer and went straight past Butch the bully, then he was gone.

Everyone was talking about it but they all got ready to run, then the sky went black and the same thing happened every night.

It was very mysterious!

The Fright for Everyone
Two weeks went by. Each day, a boy or girl disappeared. Knights went to defend the city, but of course they never came back again. Jonathan was very angry. He strolled up the hill, round a rocky mountain and through fields.

But then it went black, a stream of fire appeared in the sky, it came down like a bullet, went straight past Jonathan, and he disappeared!

The Mystery Cave and Jonathan
Jonathan was taken up into the air and something was holding him. He looked up above and saw a giant claw (about as big as a barrel) was holding him.

He looked in front and saw a cave all glittering with rubies, sapphires, diamonds, blue john and all kinds of precious stones!

Then 'BUMP!' they landed heavily. Then as he looked up to his horror he saw a DRAGON! Huge and so slimy I'd better not describe him. Jonathan's mouth was wide open. Then they started into the Cave of Crystals!

The Cave of Crystals
It was pitch black inside the cave. But as his eyes focused he could see the people that had been captured, and they were tied up in rope! And for once in his life Jonathan was scared.

Two red eyes stared at him from the darkness and a shadowy shape appeared. It formed itself into the shape of a dragon!

The Breakfast, Tea, Lunch and Dinner
The only thing I can describe are its teeth. They were as sharp as needles and as big as lamp posts.

Jonathan would be for dinner and the others for other meals.

Jonathan brought out his sword but the dragon broke it with a swipe of its claw.

He brought out everything he had except for one special battle axe. He kept that safe. One by one the knives and swords went 'Snap, snap, snap!' This battle axe was his last chance!

The Blunt Battle Axe
He heaved the battle axe at the dragon, but nothing happened! It was blunt! He was tied up with rope and the dragon flew out to claim another victim.

Now there was one dagger left in Jonathan's hand. It had snapped but he managed to cut through the rope. He let the other people go free, but the knights came with Jonathan to blast the dragon off the face of the earth; but this was not at all finished.

The Dragon Battle
Up the hills over mountains they went until they were at the village. 'What shall we do?' they asked shakily. 'I have a plan!' and he whispered it to the knights. It was the most stupendous idea. A knight stood in the city that night until the flames went past him but as they did, he swung his razor-sharp sword into the dragon's chest. There was a squeal, and it fell dead and the knight was still there.

The Dragon Family

Next day, the children were out playing, laughing and singing, and Jonathan was on a swing in the park.

The wind blew hard and then harder. Then it sent tidal waves onto the shore, Jonathan fell off his swing and cut his knee badly and he had to have a bandage on.

Then he looked outside. He had a white window. 'Mummy!' he called. 'The window's frosted up!' But it hadn't, it was not white at all, outside the window there was a claw about as big as a church.

'Wow, that's big!' he said; 'but it's another dragon and I've got a bad knee.'

The Mother Savage

The claw grabbed a school full of children and walked away to a giant tomb. It came back again and picked up an old gaffer and walked back again. Year after year went by.

And when Jonathan's knee got better, he went to a shop and bought a strong razor-blade sword and walked out.

Half way home a green dragon as big as a skyscraper came and picked him up. He went into the tomb to find a pit of fire.

'You're going there next!' said the dragon. Jonathan was still staring at the pit.

The Pit of Fire and Death

The bones were lying at the bottom of the pit and Jonathan nearly dropped his sword. His mouth was wide open, his eyes were red and his face turned blue with fright.

Then his scaredness turned to rage. 'I won't be killed!' he shouted. The dragon was so surprised she let go. Jonathan spun round and whacked the dragon's nose one hundred times until it got very angry.

The Mother Dragon is Angry

It stamped its feet and raged in terror and fell dead on the floor. 'That's two,' he said, 'I know there will be three soon.'

That day he walked home with a big crowd following him, all cheering and singing songs. The sun was shining and everyone was playing until Jonathan got married and had children of his own.

It had been a happy place for about nineteen years, but, of course, more dragons were making their way to Germany from the End of the World.

Warrior Dragon Two

The next dragon was flying as fast as light from the end of the world to Germany. It killed thousands of people. A police-man phoned Jonathan and said 'Number three, *aaaaahhhhhh.*' Jonathan jumped into his rocket car and zoomed off to Munich at a very fast 80,000 m.p.h.

He could see the giant dragon miles away. He stopped to think twice but he must save the people of Munich. The only trouble was, it was the warrior dragon, number two.

The Death of Jonathan's Family

The dragon was so big and clumsy that it looked like King Kong going mad. Jonathan rode towards it with his favourite weapon ready, but not knowing that another dragon came and had killed his family.

He launched his only rocket at one warrior dragon and it blew up into 1,000,000,000.50 pieces (it took me ten days to count them); the next dragon had been killed by the guards.

Jonathan was so sad that his family was dead, he killed all the dragons there were in the end of the world and married someone else.

DON'T MISS BOOK TWO
OF JONATHAN AND THE GOBLINS' GOLD MINE

BYE!

Mercedes Choules (13)

Ageing Days

I was five
The first time
I ran away, to rockets, up and down
seats, nature's things
I ran away to freedom
Away from babies screaming
Mum and dad, politics and
Money, listening through the keyhole,
Arguing.

I was six
The first time
I set off to a
prison camp, millions and trillions of
others, just like me,
But they were bigger
people, they said they
Would help me, but
they ordered me. Books,
pencils, rubbers, work?
Why?

I was seven
The first time
I was caught, sent
to head office, to
be punished, but
why? I only put
the things, white
things which the
bigger people use, I
put it in my pocket,
Why?

I was eight
The first time
I fell in love with
a damsel in distress,
She was one of the bigger people
than me, known
as my leader or teacher?
I stopped and caught the
cannon balls being thrown
at her, by ones like me, In
the large banqueting
hall.

Michael Freeman (8)

My Mum!

My mum knows a ghost that lives in my attic.
The attic is a cobweb for people my mum does not like.
She throws them in with the ghosts that live there.
My mum says don't worry you'll be dead in a second.

Philip W Sayers (10)

Paul Leipnik (10)

My Great Grandpa

When my Grandpa comes home
From the mill,
With ice-cold fingers
and bony, wrinkled face,
Sometimes he reads to me
of monsters at sea,
But there is something mysterious about him,
He looks at the tall grandfather clock
Watching the pendulum
Swing to and fro
And the long hands of the clock reach to
Stab the numbers like daggers.

Louise Bagshawe (13)

Lament for Bouddicca

In the eye of the Mother
In the sight of Epona of the foals
I keen.
Hear my lament for our black Queen
For our dark leader.

In Bouddicca of the Iceni dwelt
The spirit of the white wind over the grasses,
The spirit of the moon on the apple trees,
The life of the tribe.
In the Queen was the life-blood of my people.

O harpers, lament for Bouddicca.
Mourn for the warrior Queen!
Mourn for the leader of the war-host!
We shall not forget, we the horse-people, the Iceni.

Had you seen Bouddicca in her chariot
Her red cloak in the wind and a coil of gold round her neck,
Then you had seen a Queen indeed.
The Queen died in the Royal Dun.
She went to the west of the sunset
From the place where she was born.

In the eye of the Mother
In the sight of Epona of the foals
I keen.

Matilda Bagshawe (12)

Linda Turner

Linda Turner (13)
Snails

When Russell Pattison began to make a hobby of snail watching, he had no idea that his handful of specimens would become hundreds in no time. Only two months after the original snails were carried up to the Pattison study, some twenty glass tanks and bowls, all teeming with snails, lined the walls, rested on the desks and windowsills, and were beginning even to cover the floor. His mother disapproved strongly and would no longer enter the room.

At school, teachers were noticing a vast improvement in his work. He began to answer more questions, make more friends, and more importantly he stopped talking in class and began to take an interest in the work. When anyone congratulated him on his achievements, he gave all the credit to his snails. Many girls thought he was 'weird' and even the boys began to stop congratulating him.

By now Russell would not allow anyone to set foot in his study. Too many snails had the habit of crawling around on the floor, of going to sleep glued to chair bottoms and to the backs of books on the shelves. Snails spent much of their time sleeping, especially the older snails. This is one of the reasons why Russell began collecting the snails!

During the month of June, Russell was so busy with his exams that he hadn't been in his study for nearly three weeks. As soon as his mother began complaining of a stale, fishy smell he remembered about his snails; he shot upstairs and flung open the door to his study. To his shock and horror he could see three to four layers of snails all over each of the six walls in the room. He had difficulty closing the door without squashing any. The thick clusters in the corners made the room look quite round. In the middle of the ceiling stood a long stalactite, which could have formed a column if his mother had not reminded him of the the snails.

He had to do something about the ceiling, and straight away. He took a chair and scraped off all the snails he could see. Just as he was about to stand on the chair, the chandelier collapsed and hit the side of his head. He fell. 'Mother!' he screamed as he felt the snails crawl up his trousers and in his shoes. The scream, however loud it could have been, was muffled by the snails, as though he was in a soundproof room. He plucked up all his strength to reach the door but he could not see a thing amongst all the snails. He screamed 'Mother!' again, although it made no difference. Suddenly he felt a vast force pull him down. His vision grew black. He knew the snails were slowly murdering him but he did not have the force to move.

Over his nostrils then down his throat they slithered, not knowing what they were doing.

Annamary Marshall (13)

Three Wee Kings

'Come on, luv, get up,' shouted Caspar's mum. 'You'll be late for school.'

'I'm up,' came the reply. Caspar was looking up at the ceiling as he lay on his bed. He slowly got up and wandered over to the window and wiped the mist off it, first writing his name, then wiping it over with the cuff of his sleeve. The snow gently fell on Glasgow and he could hear the gritters in the distance.

Caspar turned round and looked at the small, dismal room where he slept. It was covered with posters of Celtic football players, his heroes.

'Come on, hurry up.' A shout from downstairs told him that his mum was waiting, and Caspar knew that you didn't keep his mum waiting.

He quickly got dressed into his best trousers and his clean blue shirt, his tie and his grey jumper – with the hole in the arm. He ran downstairs, where his mum was waiting.

'Quick! Eat up your breakfast!' Caspar's mum was rushing about frantically, while his father sat watching Breakfast TV. She was more frantic than ever today and he wondered why, then he remembered – tomorrow – how could he have forgotten?

He ate his breakfast slowly and got up, ready to go to school.

'Bye, Mum,' he said quietly.

'Oh – goodbye, dear. Wait a minute and I'll give you some money.'

At this, she raked around in her bag and brought out 10p. 'Oh, I'm sorry, luv, but that's all I can give you.'

Caspar nodded and went out of the door, still thinking about tomorrow. As he walked along he met his friends, Baltassar and Melchior. They said hello but nothing more. There was nothing else to say. The three boys were all thinking about something else as they trudged along. Caspar was thinking about the contest, Baltassar about the party and Melchior about the circus, but they were all thinking about something else – tomorrow.

There was a very steep hill on the way to school, but they did not run down. A poor old lady was trying desperately to get up the hill, and, oh, what fun it would have been to push her down again when she got halfway up. She was carrying a box of groceries and was shivering with the cold. Instead of pushing her, they helped her up the hill. The lady was surprised, but glad of the help. When they got up the hill she thanked them. Unfortunately because of their good deed they were late for school, but the teacher did not shout at them. How could she – because of tomorrow.

All through the day they could not think of anything else but tomorrow. Melchior sat looking at the clock, half past three, that meant drawing. Melchior drew what he wanted for Christmas, Baltassar drew a Christmas tree, but Caspar could not think of anything to draw; all he did was look out of the window. It was getting dark and he noticed a star shining in the empty sky. He decided to draw that. The star seemed to say, 'Come, please come.' But Caspar did not know why.

Then the bell rang and children ran from the school as if it were on fire, jumping and dancing and playing, but not those three. No, they wandered along feeling sorry for themselves. As they went along they passed the football stadium; Caspar sighed. They went on further and passed the circus tent; Melchior sighed. Then they passed a big house; Baltassar sighed. Finally, they were at their houses. They said farewell and went in.

Caspar wiped his feet on the mat and went in quietly.

'Is that you, dear?'

'Aye, Mum.'

'Good, did you have a nice day?'

'Aye, Mum – is Dad in?'

'No, dear, he's out on shift, he won't be in till eleven o'clock.'

'Is my dinner ready?'

'Yes, dear, have you got any homework?'

'No, not today.'

'Oh, yes, because of tomorrow.'

'Aye, that's right. I'll get changed now, OK?'

'Yes, dear.'

Caspar went up stairs to get changed, while his mother put out his dinner on the only table in the house. The TV was off and the house was silent except for the boiler rumbling. Caspar was to have a bath for tomorrow.

After he had changed, he had his dinner and then had a bath.

It was eight o'clock and Caspar had just had his bath. He had decided to go upstairs to his room. He sat looking out of the window and saw the star again. He knew it was the same one because it was shining brighter than any other star. It still seemed to say, 'Come, please come.' He turned away and got into bed.

In the morning he awoke with a sinking feeling. Today was the day. As it was Saturday he could have a lie in. It was about ten o'clock and he could hear his father snoring very loudly and saying things in his sleep. He got up and went downstairs.

'Oh, hello, luv, have a good sleep?' asked his mother cheerfully.

'Aye, thanks.'

'Do you want your breakfast?'

'Aye, please.'

'It's your big day, are you excited?'

'Aye, just a little.'

'Oh, I'll be there to see you, you'll like that, won't you?'

'Aye,' he said quietly and then uncrossed his fingers from behind his back.

'Now then, are you going out to play today?'

'No, not today.'

'Oh, well.'

There was a long silence and then Caspar said, 'Can I have my breakfast?'

His mum laughed and went into the small kitchen to make him something. She was happy all day, even when Caspar's dad came down.

Finally, it was evening. His mother was away out and she had left the new white vest and socks, as he knew she would and he was ready.

'I'll be going, then.'

'Good lad,' his father said. 'Goodbye.'

'Goodbye, Dad. I suppose you'll be going to the football match?'

'Aye, I will.'

'Then you'll tell me. . .'

'Och, you'll see it on TV. On you go.'

Caspar went out and he met up with his friends. All of them were carrying a present. Caspar looked up in the sky. There was the star shining brighter than ever, as if it were proud of them; and this time it seemed to say, 'Thank you, thank you!'

The snow covered Glasgow. It was a picture for anyone's eyes. In the distance three small figures trudged along following a star, which stopped at a place where they saw a baby and, as they bent down and bowed and gave their presents of gold, frankincense and myrrh, there was a burst of applause, people cheering and clapping, cameras flashing and then the curtains closed.

The teacher said, 'Thank you, boys and girls, that was a wonderful nativity play.'

Irene Neophytou (7)
Mr Winter

Once upon a time there lived a woman. She had a son and one daughter. Their mother was very ill. The children had to look after her. They had to bring her food upstairs to her bedroom. They phoned the doctor to see what was wrong with her, but the doctor did not know what was wrong with her. So he said to the children to look after your mother very carefully. I am very sorry I do not know what is wrong with your mother said the doctor. And said goodbye children.

The children's names were Sam and Michelle. They had to look after their mother very carefully, or she might die. Sam and Michelle were very sad they did not know what to do, they did not go to school because they were worried. They knew that their mother would die. They just had a feeling that their mother would die. One night when Sam and Michelle were sleeping their mother died, because of her illness. The next morning Sam and Michelle were very sad, and started to cry. Their father said don't cry, let's go and bury her. So they went on a horse to bury her. They prayed to good Lord to bless her soul. The next day their neighbours came and said don't cry my dears, people do not live for ever. A few weeks later their father bought a stepmother. It was winter and the children were cold. The stepmother was very kind to them at first. The children lived very happy for a few years. Always thinking of their dead mother.

One day Sam went out in the garden to play with Michelle. They played quite happily until a snake came. Sam and Michelle were very frightened and screamed and shouted Father, Father, a snake's coming and they moved back. Their father came with a stick and started to hit the snake but it was no good. The snake bit him, he did not know what to do. The snake was poisoned, after two moments he was dead. The children said oh, no, not another one dead. The stepmother was horrified when she saw Sam's and Michelle's father on the ground, dead. She said oh, no, you stupid children. Look what you've done, you've made your father die. And she started to shout at them. She said for this you will have no dinner for your supper. I do not want to see your faces, go to your rooms, go to sleep. She said. When they were in their rooms they did not go to sleep because they were hungry.

Mr Winter was a very kind man, he had a wife and they did not have no children. They had a lovely cottage and a lovely garden that grew strawberries, nothing but strawberries and trees. He had been spying on the stepmother and heard what she had said. When the stepmother was not looking, he went and bought some dinner and crept in, went upstairs to Sam's and Michelle's bedroom. When he got there he said, children, don't worry, I have got some dinner for you, here, eat it. I will tell you why I have bought you some dinner and he told them how he had heard their stepmother and how he had seen the snake and how they called their father and how their father got bitten. When Sam and Michelle had finished he told them do you want to leave this stepmother, the children said yes in excitement and went with Mr Winter to his cottage. The stepmother was sleeping and so they crept down the stairs not to wake her up. When they got to Mr Winter's cottage he showed them his cottage and all the rooms inside it. Then he gave them some pyjamas showed them their room and they slept because they were tired. The next morning the stepmother was very happy to get rid of them.

Mr Winter looked after them like his own children. They were very happy. They lived happily ever after. God help them.

Sara Grimes (8)

The Mysterious Boat Trip

One day a bomb landed on the area around London. It even blew up our little Larkhall and Swainswick. The school guinea pigs ran away. For they can run very fast, and got to a place with lots of grass and dandelions and clover (Paradise). But I thought this was my lucky day. Now I can get away from bossy old Mum and Dad. So I got my blue swimming bag, my swimming stuff, some wendy house, a gatway pizza or 2, a packet of biscuits, 5 apples, my jumpsuit, my toothpaste, toothbrush, my nighty, 3 batteries, my bow and arrows (I could eat with my fingers), and a torch. I borrowed Boubsey's trailer, and set off with Lizzie, Katie and Boubsey, on bikes. You may picture it. 2 3-wheelers and 2 2-

wheelers. I brought a map. Just as the bomb landed we got out of Larkhall. By the time we got to Bristol it was getting dark. But I said to them 'We should carry on, because the more we go the sooner we'll make the sea and get to that big boat that's been promised.' So we set off again. By the time we were nearly out of Bristol, it was dark so we set up my wendy house and had a good night's sleep.

In the morning we set off again. Most of Bristol was blown up so we could have lots of space. No one spotted us, and we were soon out of Bristol. We were now nearing the sea. You could see it and its waves, looking like a grey strip of sky in the distance. In about a quarter of an hour we were at the harbour. (This was spring 1986, and I was 10, 11.5.85) It was a warm day, so the sea had a pleasant breeze, just right for a large boat. When we got there the boat was there, ready and waiting. It had one cabin, and was about as big as the classroom, so there was plenty of room. As I had 400 quid we got some furniture from a dutch auction and got a small mattress and 3 big ones for only 5 quid. Then we got 10 blankets for only 3 quid, and then a little table about as big as one of our school tables which costed only 90p and some stools which costed 1 quid, and 3 pictures which costed 95p. We got some things from the dump, too. Then we set off. I did not know how to drive boats but when I tried I did. So we set off, and the first place we came to was a rock. It was a large rock, about half the size of the school grounds. There were 10 trees, so we found some wood, set up a house, put up some boxes and had a meal.

The next day was a windy day. We woke up and saw the boat floating away. I put on my swimming costume, and dived into the sea. It was about as cold as Cleveland Baths swimming pool, but I didn't care. I swam out, and found our boat, but now a new problem arose. I couldn't get the boat back. The others couldn't be bothered to come out, and Boubsey couldn't swim without his polyota on. But what about me? I couldn't stay in the water much longer without freezing. Or drowning. Then I had an idea. I swam back and got a rope. I threw it back and it caught on the railings. I pulled myself up. Then I got in and drove back to the rock. 'We betta get a move on,' said Lizzie. 'I saw a big ship coming towards us.' 'Yes,' I said. 'Our house will be searched, and if we're found we'll be taken to an orphanage.' So we locked our house, and took all our belongings out of our hut and set out in our boat at 30mph.

Soon we saw lots of people crowd onto our island. 'I'm glad we got away in time,' I said. Suddenly we saw a ship steaming towards us at 20 mph. We accelerated, 40, 50, 60 mph. At last we came to a point where the other boat ran out of fuel, and went away. We sailed on till we came to France. I said we should stop and get some food and fuel, but not scargo or hammerhacky. Boubsey thought he would try some scargo, but when he saw it was snails he changed his mind. He also wanted to try hammerhacky, but when he saw it was spiders in fimush and not a sweetie hammer hacking away at choclate wood, he changed his mind, of course. Then we set off to the tropics.

Chapter 2
The Tropical Island
It took 1 week to get to the tropical island, and a boring journey it was too. But when we got there we all loved it. It was very hot and a paradise for bored children. We had to be careful of adders and snakes and tarantulas, for such creatures lived on desert islands. The island was deserted because the fierce polooganichas lived there. The polooganichas came out at night from the caves on the island. (This is what polooganichas look like:)

I will now tell you what the polooganichas thought when they heard. The polooganichas are very deadly creatures. The polooganichas were very pleased when they heard that we had arrived. 'Ha, ha, ha,' they cried. 'Hee, Hee, Hee, Taly Tarter, vhe peoplezes has arrived, dinny times is hew angin, time for owr suppets,' they cried. 'Get out eatin stuffs for cooking wif.' 'Haly Hachit time for dinys.' So while we were putting up our tent the polooganichas were getting their odd-shaped pots and pans out. Then, as we snuggled down into our nice warm sleeping bags, the polooganichas were creeping out of their caves, and searching everywhere for our tent.

So while we were snuggling down to sleep (all except me) the polooganichas were crowding round our tent, ready to strike. The dim lights were even dimmer than usual, and though the others were all fast asleep, I was awake, for I felt like I was being watched, as indeed I was. I woke up the others and picked up my bow and walked out. The moon was shining brightly, and the sand looked like flake silver. It looked beautiful, but strange. Suddenly the shouts of war filled the air. I fired a stream of arrows and in doing so killed 20 polooganichas. Out rushed Lizzie and Katie and Boubsey, using their teeth, legs, arms and fists and nails. Along came some painted warriors, and joined in on our side. Soon all the polooganichas had fled, to their caves and underground passages. It was our side that was victorious. The painted warriors got back into their boats and rowed away. We soon cleaned the island up. Then, once we had cleaned the island up we went back to bed.

The natives had given us the island, and a horse for me and ponies for the others. And a very small, tame pony was given to Boubsey, and I gave him pony lessons about running up stirrups and putting on headcollars and staying in the saddle and brushing her with a curvy comb, and the dandy brush and all the easy things about riding, till off straightaway. I named mine Black Beauty, for it was black. I named Boubsey's one Natasha for it was a girl. I called Lizzie's Goldie, for it was a palomino. Boubsey's was brown. I named Katie's Silksie, for it was a dapple grey. For a time all went well. The horse and the ponies thrived, roaming round the island on their own, and we were very happy till the storm came. This is how it happened. We were all out having a nice time, playing with our ponies (my horse was swimming in the sea on its own), when a flash of lightning shot through the air, just missing my head. 'Back to the house,' I cried, and picking up Boubsey I ran to the hut, and shut the door so quickly Lizzie nearly got her nose caught. 'At least we are safe in here,' I said. And we were.

Benjamin White (7)
The Man by the River

One day a man was walking by a river and he looked into a waterfall. In it five little men were standing very quietly. Their eyes were like gold. The man just stared and stared. They came out of the water and started talking and that talking became singing. This what they sang:

'We are the five colour eyes.'

With a gold flash they were gone and never seen again. Well, did I say never seen again? Then I was wrong because they were seen on a lovely sunny day and about my lunch time. Their eyes were sparkling with gold. This time they sent showers of gold down on the city and the man became a very rich man.

But that wasn't the end, years passed and the man grew very old. The five men appeared the same way again. But this time their eyes were sparkling with silver and they were as young as before. The next day the man looked in the mirror and he was very young again. One day he came to a town and bought a horse and cart and went for a ride down the river. The cart crashed against a stone. As he fell he saw the five men in front of his eyes. Their eyes were flashing from gold, silver, ruby, hazel, brown and blue. He smashed his head against the ground and fell into the river and drowned. He was sitting in a bed with the five men around him. He decided that he could live for ever because of the five men.

Philippa Best (12)
Gypsy Lace

She stood there, alone, clutching her basket full of fancies,
Her hand stretched out swiftly to tell of the world's misfortune.
'Buy from a gypsy, your luck will stay.'
For a moment she hesitates and her wizened face stares into the
    sun,

Slowly, she spreads her wares about her,
'Buy from a gypsy,' her voice echoes round the empty lane.
A cloud crosses the sky and seven crows screech foreboding.
Scanning the slowly dusk-filling sky, she picks her prey,
'Buy from a gypsy,' she screams and the crows fly away into the
    dark.

Denise Spicer (12)

125

Index of Award Winners
Runners-up and Illustrators

*   Award Winners
**   Special Award Winners
Illustrators